Answers
to Prayer

Charles G. Finney's

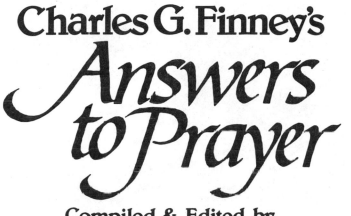

Answers to Prayer

Compiled & Edited by
Louis Gifford Parkhurst, Jr.

BETHANY HOUSE PUBLISHERS
MINNEAPOLIS, MINNESOTA 55438
A Division of Bethany Fellowship, Inc.

Published by Bethany House Publishers
A Division of Bethany Fellowship, Inc.
6820 Auto Club Road, Minneapolis, Minnesota 55438

Printed in the United States of America

Library of Congress Cataloging in Publication Data

Finney, Charles Grandison, 1792-1875.
 Answers to prayer.

 Includes bibliographical references.
 1. Prayer.   I. Parkhurst, Louis Gifford, 1946-
II. Title.
BV210.2.F53   1983   248.3'2   83-12253
ISBN 0-87123-296-0

To
My Parents
Who First Taught Me
How To Pray

CHARLES G. FINNEY was one of America's foremost evangelists. Over half a million people were converted under his ministry in an age that offered neither amplifiers nor mass communications as tools. Harvard Professor Perry Miller affirmed that "Finney led America out of the eighteenth century." As a theologian, he is best known for his *Revival Lectures* and his *Systematic Theology*.

LOUIS GIFFORD PARKHURST, JR., is pastor of First Christian Church of Rochester, Minnesota, and Instructor in Ethics/Philosophy at Minnesota Bible College. He garnered a B.A. and an M.A. from the University of Oklahoma and an M.Div. degree from Princeton Theological Seminary. He is married and the father of two children. This is his fourth Finney book.

CONTENTS

BOOKS BY CHARLES G. FINNEY
Published by Bethany House Publishers

INTRODUCTION

Answers to Prayer is the companion volume to Charles G. Finney's *Principles of Prayer*, and it has been prompted by the keen interest shown in the remarkable experiences of answered prayer in his life. During my lectures on Finney's *Principles of Prayer*, people have indicated further interest in how these principles were applied by Finney in his life and ministry. Finney discovered his principles of prayer by studying the Scriptures prayerfully, by enlightenment from the Holy Spirit, and by experiencing amazing answers to prayer.

I have carefully explored the previously unpublished, version of Finney's *Autobiography*, and from that have included previously omitted material (within brackets in the text). Some of this new material is quite startling and informative. The very interesting material on Finney's prayer life in Appendix A is from Finney's biography, written by his close friend and associate at Oberlin College, Professor G. Frederick Wright.

To help you apply what Finney discovered about prayer, I have begun each autobiographical sketch with an appropriate quotation from *Principles of Prayer*. At the conclusion of each sketch, I have asked a question to encourage you to probe more deeply what you have just read, and to possibly stimulate prayer group discussion. Each question, along with the autobiographical sketch, should drive us to prayer and to renewing our commitment to Christ and His Great Commission. Each of these sketches on answered

9

prayer contains one or more important principles which we need to recognize, relate, and apply to our lives. These would aid in prayer group discussion, confession, and revival if studied prior to each meeting by each member.

My personal prayer is that these two books of Finney's, *Principles of Prayer* and *Answers to Prayer*, will motivate each person to pray and to seek the aid of the Holy Spirit in his walk and witness. I also pray that the books of his sermons on Romans, *Principles of Victory* and *Principles of Liberty*, will communicate the truth of the Gospel to you to aid you in developing a mature faith and fruitful ministry wherever the Lord has called you to serve. I hope that these four books will be an able introduction to the deeper thoughts that many will seek in his *The Heart of Truth* and *Systematic Theology.*

I wish to give special thanks to Gordon C. Olson of Bible Research Fellowship for providing me with his personal copy of Finney's *Autobiography* as the basis for the new materials in this book. Gordon Olson spent over 150 hours making a page-by-page comparison of the 1876 printed edition with the secretarial handwritten "Memoirs in Manuscript" of over 1000 pages in the Oberlin College Library. His personal copy of the *Autobiography* contains all the important variations and additions, and the copied and typed sheets are pasted into his printed volume in their proper place. His copy also contains the material I have included on pages 108–110. I am also grateful to him for the Testimonial Letter in Appendix B, which I was happy to discover while doing research in Olson's fine collection of materials on Charles Finney.

For the sake of His Kingdom,

L. G. Parkhurst, Jr.
Christian Life Study Center
P.O. Box 7024
Rochester, Minnesota 55903
September 16, 1982

1

FIRST PRAYER MEETINGS

"Prevailing, or effectual prayer, is that prayer which attains the blessing that it seeks. It is that prayer which effectively moves God. The very idea of effectual prayer is that it affects its object."[1]

I was particularly struck with the fact that the prayers I had listened to, from week to week, were not, that I could see, answered. Indeed, I understood from their utterances in prayer, and from other remarks in their meetings, that those who offered them did not regard them as answered.

When I read my Bible, I learned what Christ had said in regard to prayer and answers to prayer. He had said, "Ask, and ye shall receive, seek and ye shall find, knock and it shall be opened unto you. For everyone that asketh receiveth, and he that seeketh findeth, and to him that knocketh it shall be opened." I read also what Christ affirms, that God is more willing to give His Holy Spirit to them that ask Him than earthly parents are to give good gifts to their children. I heard them pray continually for the outpouring of the Holy Spirit, and also as often confess that they did not receive what they asked for.

They exhorted each other to a more active witness, and to pray earnestly for revival, asserting that if they did their

---

[1]From *Principles of Prayer* by Charles G. Finney and L. G. Parkhurst, Jr. (Minneapolis: Bethany House Publishers, 1980), p. 17.

duty, prayed for the outpouring of the Holy Spirit, and were in earnest, the Spirit of God would be poured out, they would have a revival of religion, and non-Christians would be converted. But in their prayer and conference meetings, they would continually confess that they were making no progress in securing revival.

This inconsistency, the fact that they prayed so much and were not answered, was a hindrance to my own conversion. I knew not what to make of it. It was a question in my mind whether I was to understand that these persons were not truly Christians, and therefore did not prevail with God; or did I misunderstand the promises and teachings of the Bible on this subject, or was I to conclude that the Bible was not true? Here was something inexplicable to me; and it seemed to me that it would almost drive me into skepticism. It seemed to me that the teachings of the Bible did not correspond with the facts which were before my eyes.

On one occasion, when I was in one of the prayer meetings, I was asked if I did not desire that they should pray for me. I told them no, because I did not see that God answered their prayers. I said, "I suppose I need to be prayed for, for I know I am a sinner; but I do not see that it will do any good for you to pray for me, for you are continually asking, but you do not receive. You have been praying for revival ever since I have been in Adams, and yet you have it not. You have been praying for the Holy Spirit to descend upon yourselves, and yet complaining of your leanness." I recollect having used this expression at that time: "You have prayed enough since I have attended these meetings to have prayed the devil out of Adams, if there is any virtue in your prayers. But here you are praying on, and complaining still." I was quite earnest in what I said, and not a little irritable, I think, in consequence of my being brought so continually face to face with the truth; which was a new experience for me.

But on further reading of my Bible, it struck me that the

reason their prayers were not answered was because *they did not comply with the revealed conditions upon which God had promised to answer prayer. They did not pray in faith*, in the sense of expecting God to give them the things they asked for.

This thought, for some time, lay in my mind as a confused questioning, rather than in any definite form that could be stated in words. However, this relieved me, so far as questions about the truth of the Gospel were concerned; and after struggling in that way for some time, my mind became quite settled that whatever unanswered questions there might be either in my own mind or in my pastor's mind, or in the mind of the church, the Bible was, nevertheless, the true Word of God.

This being settled, I was brought face to face with the question whether I would accept Christ as presented in the Gospel or pursue my own plans and goals. At this period, my mind, as I have since known, was so deeply convicted by the Holy Spirit that I could not long leave this question unsettled; nor could I long hesitate between the two courses of life presented to me.[2]

Question for Thought and Prayer

Does my prayer life and the prayer life of my church demonstrate the reality of God and answered prayer, or do we leave the impression that prayer doesn't really do any good?

---

[2]*Autobiography*, pp. 9-11. From *Memoirs of Rev. Charles G. Finney* (New York: A. S. Barnes & Company, 1876); henceforth, *Autobiography*.

2

CONVERSION

"It is the Holy Spirit who leads Christians to understand and apply the promises of Scripture. . . . So it has been with many a Christian: while deeply engaged in prayer, he has seen passages of Scripture he never thought of before as having such appropriate application."[1]

The whole question of gospel salvation became clear to me in a manner most marvelous to me at the time. I think I then saw, as clearly as I ever have in my life, the reality and fullness of the atonement of Christ. I saw that His work was a finished work; and that instead of having or needing any righteousness of my own to recommend me to God, I had to submit myself to the righteousness of God through Christ. Gospel salvation seemed to me to be an offer of something to be accepted; and that it was full and complete; and that all that was necessary on my part was to be willing to give up my sins and accept Christ. Salvation, it seemed to me, instead of being a thing to be accomplished by my own works, was a thing to be found entirely in the Lord Jesus Christ, who presented himself before me as my God and my Savior.

But after this distinct revelation had stood for some little time before my mind, the question seemed to be put, "Will you accept it now, today?" I replied, "Yes, I will accept it today, or I will die in the attempt."

---

[1]*Principles of Prayer*, p. 62.

North of the village and over a hill lay a piece of woods in which I was in the almost daily habit of walking, more or less, when it was pleasant weather. It was now October, and the time was past for my frequent walks there. Nevertheless, instead of going to the office, I turned and directed my course toward the woods, feeling that I must be alone and away from all human eyes and ears, so that I could pour out my prayer to God.

But still my pride showed itself. As I went over the hill, it occurred to me that someone might see me and suppose that I was going away to pray. Yet probably there was not a person on earth that would have suspected such a thing had he seen me going. But so great was my pride, and so much was I possessed with the fear of man, that I recollect I crept along under the fence till I got so far out of sight that no one from the village could see me. I then penetrated into the woods, I should think a quarter of a mile, went over on the other side of the hill, and found a place where some large trees had fallen across each other, leaving an open place between. There I saw I could make a kind of closet. I crept into this place and knelt down for prayer. As I turned to go up into the woods, I remember having said, "I will give my heart to God, or I never will come down from there." I repeated this as I went up, "I will give my heart to God before I ever come down again."

But when I attempted to pray, I found that my heart would not pray. I had supposed that if I could only be where I could speak aloud without being overheard, I could pray freely. But lo! When I came to try, I could not speak; that is, I had nothing to say to God; or at least I could say but a few words, and those without heart. In attempting to pray I would hear a rustling in the leaves, as I thought, and would stop and look up to see if somebody were not coming. This I did several times.

Finally, in almost total despair, I said to myself, "I cannot pray. My heart is dead to God and will not pray." I then

reprimanded myself for having promised to give my heart
to God. [I thought I had made a rash promise that I should
be obliged to break.][2] My inward soul hung back, and there
was no going out of my heart to God. I began to feel deeply
that it was too late; that it must be that I was given up of
God and was past hope.

The thought was pressing me of the rashness of my
promise, that I would give my heart to God that day or die
in the attempt. It seemed to me as if that was binding upon
my soul, and yet I was going to break my vow. A great depression and discouragement came over me, and I felt almost too weak to stand upon my knees.

Just at that moment I again thought I heard someone
approach me, and I opened my eyes to see whether it were
so. But right there the revelation of my pride of heart, as the
great difficulty that stood in the way, was distinctly shown
to me. An overwhelming sense of my wickedness in being
ashamed to have a human being see me on my knees before
God took such powerful possession of me that I cried at the
top of my voice and exclaimed that I would not leave that
place if all the men on earth and all the devils in hell sur-
rounded me. "What!" I said, "such a degraded sinner as I
am, on my knees confessing my sins to the great and holy
God; and ashamed to have any human being, and a sinner
like myself, find me on my knees endeavoring to make my
peace with my offended God!" The sin appeared awful, infinitely awful. It totally humbled me before the Lord.[3]

Just at that point this passage of Scripture seemed to
drop into my mind with a flood of light: "Then shall ye go
and pray unto me, and I will hearken unto you. Then shall

---

[2]All portions of this book within brackets have been added
from the unpublished, unedited version of Finney's *Autobiography*.

[3]Finney discovered that pride was one of the chief obstacles to
conversion. His use of the anxious seat was designed in part to deal
with this particular sin. See especially, *Principles of Liberty*, "The
Anxious Seat," pp. 17-20.

ye seek me and find me, when ye shall search for me with all your heart." I instantly seized hold of this with my heart. I had intellectually believed the Bible before; but never had the truth been in my mind that faith was a voluntary trust instead of an intellectual state. I was as conscious of trusting at that moment in God's veracity as I was for my existence. Somehow I knew that that was a passage of Scripture, though I do not think I had ever read it. I knew that it was God's Word, and God's voice, as it were, that spoke to me. I cried to Him, "Lord, I take Thee at Thy word. Now Thou knowest that I do search for Thee with all my heart, and that I have come here to pray to Thee; and Thou hast promised to hear me."

That seemed to settle the question that I could then, that day, perform my vow. The Spirit seemed to lay stress upon that idea in the text, "When you search for me with all your heart." The question of when, that is, of the present time, seemed to fall heavily into my heart. I told the Lord that I would take Him at His word; that He could not lie; and that therefore I was sure He heard my prayer, and that He would be found of me.

He then gave me many other promises, both from the Old and the New Testament, especially some most precious promises relating to our Lord Jesus Christ. I never can, in words, make any human being understand how precious and true those promises appeared to me. I took them one after the other as infallible truth, the assertions of God who could not lie. They did not seem so much to fall into my intellect as into my heart, to be put within the grasp of the voluntary powers of my mind; and I seized hold of them, appropriated them, and fastened upon them with the grasp of a drowning man.

I continued thus to pray and to receive and appropriate promises for a long time, I know not how long. I prayed till my mind became so full that before I was aware of it, I was on my feet and almost running up the ascent toward the road. The question of my being converted had not so much as arisen to my thought; but as I went up, brushing through the leaves and bushes, I recollect saying with great emphasis, "If I am ever converted, I will preach the Gospel."

I soon reached the road that led to the village, and began to reflect upon what had happened; and I found that my mind had become most wonderfully quiet and peaceful. I said to myself, "What is this? I must have grieved the Holy Ghost entirely away. I have lost all my conviction. I'm no longer concerned about my soul. It must be that the Spirit has left me." "Why!" thought I, "I never was so far from being concerned about my own salvation in my life."[4]

Then I remembered what I said to God while I was on my knees—that I would take Him at His word; and indeed I remembered a good many things I had said, and concluded that it was no wonder the Spirit of God had left me; that for such a sinner as I was to take hold of God's Word in that way was presumptuous if not blasphemy. I concluded that in my excitement I had grieved the Holy Spirit, and perhaps committed the unpardonable sin.[5]

I walked quietly toward the village; and so perfectly quiet was my mind that it seemed as if all nature listened. It was on the 10th of October, and a very pleasant day. I had gone into the woods immediately after an early breakfast, and when I returned to the village I found it was dinner time. Yet I had been wholly unconscious of the time that had passed; it appeared to me that I had been gone

[4]Two of Finney's best sermons describe how to reach this state of the converted man: *Principles of Victory*, "Religion of the Law and the Gospel," pp. 137-145; and *Principles of Liberty*, "The Kingdom of God in Consciousness," pp. 183-194.

[5]Finney later discovered and advised such a bold use of the promises of the Scriptures on the part of the Christian: "You have Bibles; look them over, and whenever you find a promise that you can use, fasten it in your mind before you go on; and you will not get through the Book without finding out that God's promises mean just what they say" (*Principles of Prayer*, p. 54).

from the village but a short time.

But how was I to account for the peace of mind? I tried to recall my convictions to get back again the load of sin under which I had been laboring. But all sense of sin, all consciousness of present sin or guilt, had departed from me. I said to myself, "What is this, that I cannot arouse any sense of guilt in my soul, as great a sinner as I am?" I tried in vain to make myself anxious about my present state. I was so quiet and peaceful that I tried to feel concerned about that, lest it should be a result of my having grieved the Spirit away. But take any view of it I would, I could not be anxious at all about my soul and about my spiritual condition. The peace of mind was unspeakably great. I never can describe it in words. [No view that I could take, and no effort that I could make, brought back a sense of guilt, or the least concern about ultimate salvation.] The thought of God was sweet to my mind, and the most profound spiritual tranquillity had taken full possession of me. This was a great mystery; but it did not distress or perplex me.[6]

Question for Thought and Prayer

Does my prayer life and my obedience to God's Word demonstrate that I believe the Bible to be *truly* God's Word; and do I claim His promises for the totality of my life and my walk in the Holy Spirit?

---

[6]*Autobiography*, pp. 14-18.

3

MEETING JESUS

"A true Christian is active, but his activity and energy arise out of a deep sympathy with the indwelling Spirit of Christ. Christ is formed within him. The Spirit of Christ is the mighty energizing power of his soul."[1]

Just before evening of the day I gave my heart to Christ, the thought took possession of my mind that as soon as I was left alone in the new office, I would try to pray again, that I was not going to abandon my newly found faith at any rate; and therefore, although I no longer had any concern about my soul, still I would continue to pray.

By evening we got the books and furniture adjusted in the new offices; and I made up, in an open fireplace, a good fire, hoping to spend the evening alone. Just at dark Squire Wright, seeing that everything was adjusted, said good-night and went to his home. I had accompanied him to the door; and as I closed the door and turned around, my heart seemed to melt within me. All my emotions seemed to rise and flow out; and the cry of my heart was, "I want to pour my whole soul out to God." The rising of my soul was so great that I rushed into the [counsel] room back of the front office to pray.

There was no fire and no light in the room; nevertheless it appeared to me as if it were perfectly light. As I went in and shut the door after me, it seemed as if I met the Lord

---

[1]*Principles of Prayer*, p. 94.

Jesus Christ face to face. It did not occur to me then, nor did it for some time afterward, that it was wholly a mental image. On the contrary, it seemed to me that [I met Him face to face] as I would any other man. He said nothing, but looked at me in such a manner as to humble me at His feet. I have always since regarded this as a most remarkable experience, for it seemed to me a reality, that He stood before me, and I fell down at His feet and poured out my soul to Him. I wept aloud like a child, and made such confessions as I could with my choked utterance. It seemed to me that I bathed His feet with my tears, and yet I had no distinct impression that I touched Him.

I must have continued in this state for a good while; but my mind was too much absorbed with the interview to remember anything that I said. But I know, as soon as my mind became calm enough to break off the interview, I returned to the front office and found that the fire I had made of large wood was nearly burned out. But as I turned and was about to take a seat by the fire, I received a mighty baptism of the Holy Ghost. Without any expectation of it, without ever realizing there was any such thing for me, without any recollection that I had ever heard the thing mentioned by any person in the world [at a moment entirely unexpected by me], the Holy Spirit descended upon me in a manner that seemed to go through me, body and soul. I could feel the impression, like a wave of electricity, going through and through me. Indeed it seemed to come in waves and waves of liquid love, for I could not express it in any other way. [And yet it did not seem like water, but rather of the breath of God.] I remember distinctly that it seemed to fan me, like immense wings; [and it seemed to me, as these waves passed over me, that they literally moved my hair like a passing breeze].

No words can express the wonderful love that was shed abroad in my heart. [It seemed to me that I should burst.] I wept aloud with joy and love; and I do not know but that I should say I literally shouted out the unutterable yearnings of my heart. These waves came over me, and over me, one after the other, until I cried out, "I shall die if these waves continue to pass over me!" I said [to the Lord], "Lord, I cannot bear any more"; yet I had no fear of death.

How long this baptism continued to roll over me and go through me, I do not know. But I know it was late in the evening when a member of my choir—for I was the leader of the choir—came into the office to see me. He was a member of the church. He found me in this state of loud weeping, and said to me, "Mr. Finney, is something wrong?" I could make him no answer for some time. He then said, "Are you in pain?" I gathered myself up as best I could and replied, "No, but so happy that I cannot live."[2]

Question for Thought and Prayer

Have I so surrendered my life to the Lord Jesus Christ that I know the reality of His presence in my life?

---

[2]*Autobiography*, pp. 19-21.

4

JUSTIFIED BY FAITH

"The Holy Spirit was sent into the world by the Savior to guide His people, to instruct them, and to bring things to their remembrance, as well as to convince the world of sin."[1]

When I awoke in the morning, the sun had risen and was pouring a clear light into my room. Words cannot express the impression this sunlight made upon me. Instantly the baptism I had received the night before returned upon me in the same manner. I arose upon my knees in the bed and wept aloud with joy, and remained for some time too much overwhelmed with the baptism of the Spirit to do anything but pour out my soul to God. It seemed as if this morning's baptism was accompanied with a gentle reproof, and the Spirit seemed to say to me, "Will you doubt? Will you doubt?" I cried, "No! I will not doubt: I cannot doubt." He then cleared the subject up so much to my mind that it was in fact impossible for me to doubt that the Spirit of God had taken possession of my soul.

In this state I was taught the doctrine of justification by faith as a present experience. That doctrine had never taken any such possession of my mind that I had ever viewed it distinctly as a fundamental doctrine of the Gospel. Indeed, I did not know at all what it meant in the proper sense. But I could now see and understand what was meant by the passage: "Being justified by faith, we have peace with God

---

[1]*Principles of Prayer*, p. 63.

through our Lord Jesus Christ." I could see that the moment I believed while up in the woods, all sense of condemnation had entirely left me, and that from that moment I could not feel a sense of guilt or condemnation by any effort I could make. My sense of guilt was gone; my sins were gone; and I do not think I felt any more sense of guilt than if I had never sinned.

This was just the revelation I needed. I felt myself justified by faith; and, so far as I could see, I was in a state in which I did not sin. Instead of feeling that I was sinning all the time, my heart was so full of love that it overflowed. My cup ran over with blessing and with love, and I could not feel that I was sinning against God. Nor could I recover the least sense of guilt for my past sins. Of this experience I said nothing, that I remember, at the time, to anybody; that is, of this experience of justification [and so far as I could see, of present sanctification][2].

Question for Thought and Prayer

Can I approach God in my prayers, knowing that I have been cleansed from all my sins by the shed blood of His Son, and can I claim this as a present experience, knowing that if I confess my sins He is faithful and just to forgive me of all my sins and cleanse me of all unrighteousness?[3]

---

[2]*Autobiography*, pp. 22, 23. A comprehensive definition of justification and sanctification is in *Finney's Systematic Theology* (Minneapolis: Bethany House Publishers, 1976). The following summary is taken from that book: "The disinterested and infinite love of God, the Father, Son, and Holy Spirit, is the true and only foundation of the justification and salvation of sinners. . . . A sanctifying faith unites the believer to Christ as his justification; but be it always remembered, that no faith receives Christ as a justification, that does not receive Him as a sanctification, to reign within the heart. . . . To sanctify one's self is voluntarily to set one's self apart, to consecrate one's self to God. . . . Nothing is

acceptable to God, as a condition of justification, and of consequent salvation, but a repentance that implies a return to full obedience to the moral law. . . . This obedience is not rendered independent of the grace of God, but is induced by the indwelling Spirit of Christ received by faith, and reigning in the heart. . . . Justification . . . consists not in the law pronouncing the sinner just, but in his being ultimately, governmentally treated as if he were just; that is, it consists in a governmental decree of pardon or amnesty . . . upon the conditions of atonement, repentance, faith . . . present sanctification, in the sense of present full consecration to God, . . . and perseverance in faith and obedience" (337, 326, 327, 338, 339, 319, 320, 327, 328; see especially 332, 333 for a good succinct summary of Justification).

[3]Finney wrote in his *Principles of Prayer*: "Confess and forsake your sins. God will never lead you as one of His hidden ones and let you into His secrets unless you confess and forsake your sins," p. 73.

5

HIS FIRST CONVERSIONS

"If your feelings are truly benevolent, you are to consider it as the Holy Spirit leading you to pray for things according to the will of God."[1]

I spoke with many persons that day, and I believe the Spirit of God made lasting impressions upon every one of them.[2] I cannot remember one whom I spoke with who was not soon after converted. Just at evening I called at the house of a friend, where a young man lived who was employed in distilling whiskey. The family had heard that I had become a Christian; and as they were about to sit down to tea, they urged me to sit down and take tea with them. The man of the house and his wife were both professing Christians. But a sister of the lady, who was present, was an unconverted girl; and this young man of whom I have spoken, a distant relative of the family, was a professed Universalist.

I sat down with them to tea, and they requested me to ask a blessing. Though I had never prayed like this before, I did not hesitate a moment, but commenced to ask the blessing of God as we sat around the table. I had scarcely more than begun before the condition of these young people came before my mind. I felt such compassion for them that I burst into weeping and was unable to proceed. Everyone

---

[1] *Principles of Prayer*, p. 69.
[2] This was the *first* day after Finney's conversion.

around the table sat speechless for a short time, while I continued to weep. Directly, the young man moved back from the table and rushed out of the room. He fled to his room and locked himself in, and was not seen again till the next morning when he came out thoroughly converted to Christ. He has been for many years an able minister of the Gospel.

At evening, without any appointment having been made that I could learn, I observed that the people were going to the place where they usually held their conference and prayer meetings. My conversion had created a good deal of astonishment in the village. I afterward learned that some time before this some members of the church had proposed, in a church meeting, to make me a particular subject of prayer, and that Mr. Gale had discouraged them, saying that he did not believe I would ever be converted, that from conversing with me he had found that I was very much informed upon the subject of Christianity, and very much hardened.[3] And furthermore, he said he was almost discouraged; that I led the choir and taught the young people sacred music; and that they were so much under my influence that he did not believe they would ever be converted while I remained in Adams.

However, with one consent, the people seemed to rush to the place of worship. I went there myself. The minister was there, and nearly all the important people in the village. No one seemed ready to open the meeting, but the house was packed to the utmost capacity. I did not wait for anybody, but arose and began by saying that I then knew that Christianity was true. I went on and told such parts of my experience as it seemed important for me to tell.

As soon as I had finished speaking, Mr. Gale, the minister, arose and made a confession. He said he believed he had been in the way of the church, and then confessed that

---

[3]Mr. Gale, a graduate of Princeton Theological Seminary, was the minister of the church Finney attended.

he had discouraged the church when they had proposed to pray for me. He said also that when he had heard that day that I was converted, he had promptly said he did not believe it. He said he had no faith. He spoke in a very humble manner.

I had never made a prayer in public. But soon after Mr. Gale was through speaking, he called on me to pray. I did so, and think I had a good deal of liberty in prayer. We had a wonderful meeting that evening; and, from that day, we had a meeting every evening for a long time.

As I had been a leader among the young people, I immediately appointed a meeting for them, which they all attended; that is, all of the class with which I was acquainted. I gave up my time to labor for their conversion, and the Lord blessed every effort that was made in a very wonderful manner. They were converted one after another with great rapidity, and the work continued among them until only one of their number was left unconverted.

After a short time, I went down to Henderson where my father lived, and visited him. He was an unconverted man; and only one of the family, my youngest brother, had ever made a profession of Christ. My father met me at the gate and said, "How do you do, Charles?" I replied, "I am well, Father, body and soul. But, Father, you are an old man; all your children are grown up and have left your house; and I never heard a prayer in my father's house." Father dropped his head, and burst into tears, and replied, "I know it, Charles; come in and pray yourself."

We went in and engaged in prayer. My father and mother were greatly moved, and in a very short time thereafter they were both hopefully converted. I do not know that my mother had had a secret hope before; but if so, none of the family, I believe, ever knew it.[4]

---

[4]*Autobiography*, pp. 26-30.

Questions for Thought and Prayer

Since my own conversion and total commitment to Christ and His service, have I labored in prayer and in sharing the truth of the Gospel with those who do not know Christ, but who are closest to me, whom I have a great influence with because of our past relationships? Can I begin now to pray and labor for the salvation of those I love nearest me?

6

SUPERNATURAL LIGHT

"He [the Holy Spirit] prays for us by inspiring our minds. Not that He immediately suggests to us words, or guides our language, but He enlightens our minds and makes the truth take hold of our souls. He leads us to a deep consideration of the . . . state of things; . . . and the result of this is deep inspiration and yearning."[1]

Toward spring the older members of the church began to lose their zeal. I had been in the habit of rising early in the morning and spending time in prayer alone in the meetinghouse. I finally succeeded in interesting a considerable number of brethren to meet me there in the morning for a prayer meeting. This was at a very early hour, and we were generally together long before it was light enough to see to read. I persuaded my minister to attend these morning meetings. But soon they all began to be remiss.

One morning I had made several calls on the brethren, and when I returned to the meetinghouse only a few of them had gotten there. Mr. Gale was standing at the door, and as I came up all at once the glory of God shone upon and round me in a manner most marvelous. The day was just beginning to dawn. All at once a light perfectly ineffable shone in my soul and almost leveled me to the ground. In this light it seemed as if I could see that all nature praised and worshiped God except man. This light seemed to be like the

---

[1]*Principles of Prayer*, p. 60.

brightness of the sun in every direction. It was too intense for the eyes. I remembered casting my eyes down and breaking into a flood of tears in view of the fact that mankind did not praise God. I think I knew something then, by actual experience, of that light that prostrated Paul on his way to Damascus. It was surely a light such as I could not have endured long.

When I burst into such a weeping, Mr. Gale said, "What is the matter, brother Finney?" I could not tell him. I found that he had seen no light, and that he saw no reason why I should be in such a state of mind. I therefore said little. I believe I merely replied that I saw the glory of God, and that I could not endure to think of the manner in which He was treated by men. Indeed, it did not seem to me at the time that the vision of His glory was to be described in words. I wept it out, and the vision passed away and left my mind calm.

I used to have many seasons of communing with God which I cannot describe in words. And many times those seasons would end in an impression on my mind like this: "Go, see that thou tell no man." I did not understand this at the time, and several times I paid no attention to this injunction, but tried to tell my Christian brethren what communications the Lord had made to me, or rather what kind of communion I had with Him. But I soon found that it was useless to tell my brethren what was passing between the Lord and my soul. They could not understand it. They would look surprised, and sometimes I thought, incredulous. I soon learned to keep quiet in regard to those divine manifestations and say little about them.

I used to spend a great deal of time in prayer; sometimes, literally praying "without ceasing." I also found it profitable and felt very much inclined to hold frequent days of private fasting. On those days I would seek to be entirely alone with God.

Sometimes I would pursue a wrong course in fasting and

attempt to examine myself according to the ideas of self-examination then entertained by my minister and the church. I would try to look into my own heart in an attempt to examine my feelings, and would turn my attention particularly to my motives and the state of my mind. When I pursued this course, I found invariably that the day would close without any perceptible advance being made. Afterward I saw clearly why this was so. Turning my attention, as I did, from the Lord Jesus Christ and looking into myself, examining my motives and feelings, my feelings all subsided of course. But whenever I fasted and let the Spirit take His own course with me, and gave myself up to let Him lead me and instruct me, I universally found it in the highest degree useful. I found I could not live without enjoying the presence of God; and if at any time a cloud came over me, I could not rest, I could not study, I could not attend to anything with the least satisfaction or benefit until the medium was again cleared between my soul and God.[2]

Questions for Thought and Prayer

Why do I seek a deeper and more personal relationship with God? Do I intend to tell others of my experiences? Am I always checking my spiritual pulse? Or do I seek to praise God and focus on Jesus that I might be empowered to know Him and witness for Him?

---

[2]*Autobiography*, pp. 33-36.

7

ASSURANCE IN PRAYER

"If we find, by comparing our conscious, present burden with the Bible, that we are led by the Spirit to pray for an individual, we have good evidence to believe that God is prepared to bless him."[1]

The Lord taught me, in those early days of my Christian experience, many very important truths regarding the spirit of prayer. Not long after I was converted, a woman with whom I had boarded was taken very sick. She was not a Christian, but her husband claimed to be one. He came into our office one evening, being a brother of Squire Wright, and said to me, "My wife cannot live through the night." This seemed to drive an arrow, as it were, into my heart. [I felt something almost like a cramp seizing me in the region of my heart.] It came upon me in the sense of a burden that crushed me [and a kind of inward spasm], the nature of which I could not at all understand; but with it came an intense desire to pray for that woman. The burden was so great that I left the office almost immediately and went up to the meetinghouse to pray for her. There I struggled, but could not say much. I could only groan with groanings as loud and deep [as would have been impossible, I think, for me, had it not been for that terrible pressure on my mind].

I stayed a considerable time in the church in this state of mind, but got no relief. I returned to the office, but I could

---

[1]*Principles of Prayer*, p. 65.

not sit still. I could only walk the room and agonize. I returned to the meetinghouse again and went through the same process of struggling. For a long time I tried to get my prayer before the Lord, but somehow words could not express it. I could only groan and weep, without being able to express what I wanted in words. I returned to the office again and still found I was unable to rest. I returned a third time to the meetinghouse. At this time the Lord gave me power to prevail. I was enabled to roll the burden upon Him, and I obtained the assurance in my mind that the woman would not die, and indeed she would never die in her sins.

I returned to the office. My mind was perfectly quiet, and I soon left and retired to rest. Early the next morning the husband came into the office and smiling said, "She's alive, and to all appearance better this morning." I replied, "She will not die with this sickness; you may rely upon it. And she will never die in her sins." I do not know how I was made sure of this; but it was in some way made plain to me, so that I had no doubt that she would recover. She did recover, and soon after she became a Christian.

At first I did not understand this exercise of mind that I passed through. But shortly after in relating it to a Christian brother, he said to me, "Why, that was the travail of your soul."[2] A few minutes conversation and pointing me to certain Scriptures gave me to understand what it was.[3]

---

[2]Finney later wrote, "Do not deceive yourselves into thinking that you offer effectual prayer without this intense desire for a blessing. . . . Prayer is not effectual unless it is offered up with an agony of desire. The Apostle Paul speaks of it as a travail of the soul." (*Principles of Prayer*, p. 31).

[3]*Autobiography*, pp. 36, 37.

Questions for Thought and Prayer

For whom and for what things do I pray long and hard and often—for myself and for things that benefit me? Am I willing to commit myself to the Holy Spirit's leading to the point that I am willing to pray often and intensely for someone I hardly know?

8

PATIENCE IN PRAYER

"You must persevere. You are not to pray for a thing once and then cease, and call that the prayer of faith."[1]

I have spoken of one young woman as belonging to the class of young people of my acquaintance, who remained unconverted. This attracted a good deal of attention, and there was much conversation among Christians about her case. She was naturally a charming girl and very much informed on the subject of religion, but she remained unconverted.

One of the elders of the church and I agreed to make her a daily subject of prayer, to continue to present her case to the Lord, morning, noon, and evening, until she was converted. I found myself greatly burdened about her and more and more burdened as I continued to pray for her. I soon found, however, that the elder who had entered into this arrangement with me was losing prayerful concern for her. But this did not discourage me. I continued to hold on relentlessly. I also availed myself of every opportunity to converse plainly and searchingly with her on the subject of her salvation.

After I had continued in this way for some time, one evening I called to see her just as the sun was setting. As I came up to the door, I heard a shriek from a female voice, and a scuffling and confusion inside the door. I stood and

_____
[1]*Principles of Prayer*, p. 56.

waited for the confusion to be over. The lady of the house soon came and opened the door, and held in her hand a portion of a book, which had evidently been torn in two. She was pale and very much agitated. She held out that portion of the book which she had in her hand, and said, "Mr. Finney, don't you think my sister has become a Universalist?" The book was a defense of Universalism. Her sister had discovered her reading it in a private way and had tried to get it away from her; and it was the struggle to obtain that book which I had heard.

I received the information at the door; whereupon I declined to go in. It struck me very much in the same way as had the announcement that the sick woman, already mentioned, was about to die. It loaded me down with great agony. As I returned to my room, at some distance from that house, I felt almost as if I should stagger under the burden that was on my mind. I struggled, and groaned, and agonized, but could not present the case before God in words, only in groans and tears.

It seemed to me that the discovery that that young woman, instead of being converted, was becoming a Universalist so astounded me that I could not break through with my faith and get hold of God in reference to her case. There seemed to be a darkness hanging over the question, as if a cloud had risen up between me and God in regard to prevailing for her salvation.

However, I was obliged to retire that night without having prevailed. But as soon as it was light I awoke; and the first thought that I had was to beseech the God of grace again for that young woman. I immediately arose and fell upon my knees. No sooner was I upon my knees than the darkness gave way, and the whole subject opened to my mind; and as soon as I pled for her, God said to me, "Yes! yes!" *If He had spoken with an audible voice, it would not have been more distinctly understood than was this word spoken within my soul.* It instantly relieved all my anxiety.

My mind became filled with the greatest peace and joy. I felt a complete certainty that her salvation was secure.

I was incorrect, however, regarding time; which indeed was not a thing particularly impressed upon my mind at the time of my prayer. Still I expected her to be converted immediately, but she was not. She remained in her sins for several months.[2]

Question for Thought and Prayer

Do I get discouraged and give up in witnessing and in praying for another's conversion if he does not come to faith and repent of his sins in *my* time?

---

[2]*Autobiography*, pp. 37-39.

9

A FATEFUL REFUSAL

"Prayer, to be effectual, must be by the intercession of the Spirit. You never can expect to offer prayer according to the will of God without the Spirit."[1]

Soon after I was converted, the man with whom I had been boarding for some time, who was a magistrate and one of the principal men in the place, was deeply convicted of sin. He had been elected a member of the legislature of the state. I was praying daily for him and urging him to give his heart to God. His conviction became very deep; but still, from day to day, he refused, and did not become a Christian. My burden for him increased.

One afternoon several of his political friends had a protracted interview with him. On the evening of the same day, I attempted again to pray for him, as my concern for his conversion had become very great. In my prayer I had drawn very near to God. I do not remember ever to have been in more intimate communion with the Lord Jesus Christ than I was then. Indeed, His presence was so real that I was bathed in tears of joy, and gratitude, and love; and in this state of mind I attempted to pray for this friend. But the moment I did so, my mouth was shut. I found it impossible to pray a word for him. The Lord seemed to say to me, "No! I will not hear." An anguish seized upon me; I thought at first it was a temptation. But the door was shut

---

[1]*Principles of Prayer*, p. 30.

in my face. It seemed as if the Lord said to me, "Speak no more to me of that matter." It pained me beyond words. I did not know what to make of it.

The next morning I saw him; and as soon as I brought up the question of submission to God, he said to me, "Mr. Finney, I will not discuss it until I return from the legislature. I stand committed to my political friends to carry out certain measures in the legislature that are incompatible with my first becoming a Christian. And I have promised that I will not discuss the subject until after I have returned from Albany."

From the moment of that exercise the evening before, I had no burden of prayer for him at all. As soon as he told me what he had done, I understood it. I could see that his convictions were all gone, and that the Spirit of God had left him. From that time he grew more careless and hardened than ever.

When the time arrived he went to the legislature, and in the spring he returned an almost insane Universalist. I say almost insane, because instead of having formed his opinions from any evidence or course of argument, he told me this: "I have come to that conclusion, not because I have found it taught in the Bible, but because such a doctrine is so opposed to the carnal mind. It is a doctrine so generally rejected and spoken against as to prove that it is distasteful to the carnal or unconverted mind." This was astonishing to me. But everything else that I could get out of him was as wild and absurd as this. He remained in his sins, finally fell into moral decay, and died at last, as I have been told, a dilapidated man and in the full faith of his Universalism.[2]

Question for Thought and Prayer

Do I really seek to know Christ in my prayers so as to know whom and what I can rightly pray for according to the leading of the Spirit of God?

---

[2]*Autobiography*, pp. 39-41.

10

REFUSING PRAYER
AND CHOOSING A DESTINY

"If you are filled with the Spirit, . . . you will be calm under affliction. . . . You will be resigned in death; you will always feel prepared to die and not afraid to die; and after death you will be proportionately more happy in heaven."[1]

There was an old man in Evans Mills, who was not only a non-Christian, but very critical toward Christianity. He was very angry at the revival movement. I heard every day of his threatenings and blaspheming, but chose to ignore it. He refused altogether to attend any meetings. But in the midst of his opposition, and when his anger was greatest, while sitting one morning at the table, he suddenly fell out of his chair with a stroke. A physician was immediately called, who, after a brief examination, told him that he could live but a very short time and that if he had anything to say, he must say it at once. He had just strength and time, as I was informed, to stammer out, "Don't let Finney pray over my corpse." This was the last of his opposition in that place.

During that revival my attention was called to a sick woman in the community, who had been a member of a Baptist church, and was well known in the place, but people were unsure of her true spiritual condition. She was fast failing with tuberculosis and they begged me to call

---

[1]*Principles of Prayer*, p. 89.

and see her. I went, and had a long conversation with her. She told me a dream which she had when she was a girl, which made her think that her sins were forgiven. She had settled all her hopes upon that dream, and no argument convinced her otherwise. I tried to persuade her that there was no evidence of her conversion in that dream. I told her plainly that her acquaintances affirmed that she had never lived a Christian life, and had never evinced a Christian disposition; and I had come to try to persuade her to give up her false hope and see if she would not now accept Jesus Christ that she might be saved. I dealt with her as kindly as I could, but did not fail to make her understand what I meant. But she took great offense, and after I went away, complained that I tried to take away her hope and distress her mind. She died not long afterward. But her death has often reminded me of Dr. Nelson's book, *The Cause and Cure of Infidelity*. As this woman approached death, her eyes were opened; and before she left the world, she seemed to have such a glimpse of the character of God, of what heaven was, and of the holiness required to dwell there that she shrieked with agony, and exclaimed that she was going to hell. In this state, as I was informed, she died.

When still at Evans Mills, one afternoon a Christian brother called on me and wished me to visit his sister, who, as he informed me, was fast failing with tuberculosis and was a Universalist. Her husband, he said, was a Universalist and had led her into Universalism. He said he had not asked me to go to see her when her husband was at home, because he feared that he would be abusive, as he was determined that his wife should not be disturbed on the question of universal salvation. I went, and found her not at all at rest in her views of Universalism; and during my conversation with her, she gave up these views entirely and appeared to embrace the Gospel of Christ. I believe she held fast to this hope in Christ till she died.[2]

---

[2]*Autobiography*, pp. 67, 68.

Question for Thought and Prayer

Am I willing to make the commitment in prayer and under the Holy Spirit's leading to discuss salvation with all that are in need of the Gospel of Christ, regardless of their situation or nearness to death?

11

THE YOUNG PEOPLE AND REVIVAL

"The Holy Spirit gives to Christians a spiritual discern-ment respecting the movements and developments of Provi-dence. . . . There is no doubt that a Christian may be made to discern clearly the signs of the times, so as to under-stand, by Providence, what to expect, and thus to pray for it in faith."[1]

In Adams, in the spring of the year, the older members of church began greatly to decline in their witness and zeal for God. This greatly oppressed me, as it did also the young converts. About this time I read in a newspaper an article, "A Revival Revived." The substance of it was that in a cer-tain place there had been a revival during the winter; that in the spring it declined; and that upon earnest prayer be-ing offered for the continued outpouring of the Spirit, the revival was powerfully revived. This article greatly bur-dened my heart.

I was at that time boarding with Mr. Gale, and I took the article to him. I was so overcome with a sense of the di-vine goodness in hearing and answering prayer, and with a felt assurance that He would hear and answer prayer for the revival of His work in Adams, that I went through the house weeping aloud like a child. Mr. Gale seemed surprised at my feelings and my expressed confidence that God would

---

[1]*Principles of Prayer*, p. 66.

revive His work. The article made no such impression on him as it did on me.

At the next meeting of the young people, I proposed that we should observe a closet concert of prayer for the revival of God's work; that we should pray at sunrise, at noon, and at sunset, in our closets, and continue this for one week, when we should come together again and see what more could be done. No other means were used for the revival of God's work. But the spirit of prayer was immediately poured out wonderfully upon the young converts. Before the week was out I learned that some of them, when they would attempt to observe this time of prayer, would lose all their strength and be unable to rise to their feet or even stand upon their knees in their closets, and that some would lie prostrate on the floor and pray with unutterable groanings for the outpouring of the Spirit of God.

The Spirit was poured out, and before the week ended all the meetings were crowded and there was as much interest in spiritual things, I think, as there had been at any time during the revival.

And here, I am sorry to say, a mistake was made, or, perhaps I should say, a sin committed, by some of the older members of the church, which resulted in great evil. As I afterward learned, a considerable number of the older people resisted this new movement among the young converts. They were jealous of it. They did not know what to make of it, and felt that the young converts were getting out of their place, in being so forward and so urgent upon the older members of the church. This state of mind finally grieved the Spirit of God. [After I left Adams the state of religion ran down. Brother Gale, their minister, was soon dismissed, being out of health. He went away to Western, Oneida County, N.Y., and went on a farm to see if it would not restore his health.] It was not long before alienations began to rise among their older members of the church, which finally resulted in great evil to those who had allowed themselves to resist this latter revival.

The young people held out well. The converts, so far as I know, were almost universally sound, and have been thoroughly efficient Christians.[2]

Question for Thought and Prayer

Have you so opened your life to God the Holy Spirit so as to be able to see His providential working in life around you, and in what some would simply call "chance happenings"?

---

[2]*Autobiography*, pp. 44, 45.

12

GOD'S SCHOOL FOR PRAYER

"Entire consecration to God is indispensable to the prayer of faith. You must live a holy life, and consecrate all to God—your time, talents, influences—all you have, all you are, to be His entirely"[1]

The presbytery was finally called together at Adams to examine me; and, if they could agree to do so, to license me to preach the Gospel. This was in March 1824. . . . When they had examined me, they voted unanimously to license me to preach. . . .

At this meeting of presbytery I first saw the Rev. Daniel Nash, who is generally known as "Father Nash." He was a member of the presbytery. A large congregation was assembled to hear my examination. I got in a little late and saw a man standing in the pulpit speaking to the people, as I supposed. He looked at me, I observed, as I came in, and was looking at others as they passed up the aisles.

As soon as I reached my seat and listened, I observed that he was praying. I was surprised to see him looking all over the house, as if he were talking to the people, while in fact he was praying to God. Of course it did not sound to me much like prayer, and he was at that time indeed in a very cold and backslidden state. . . .

Later, I again saw Father Nash, the man who prayed with his eyes open, at the meeting of presbytery when I was

---

[1]*Principles of Prayer*, p. 56.

licensed. After he was at presbytery he became ill with inflamed eyes, and for several weeks was shut up in a dark room. He could neither read nor write, and, as I learned, gave himself up almost entirely to prayer. His own life had been radically revived, and as soon as he was able to see, with a double black veil before his face, he departed on an evangelistic trip.

When he came to Evans Mills, he was full of the power of prayer. He was another man altogether from what he had been at any former period of his Christian life. I found that he had "a praying list," as he called it, of the names of persons whom he made subjects of prayer every day, and sometimes many times a day. And praying with him, and hearing him pray in meeting, I found that his gift of prayer was wonderful and his faith almost miraculous.

There was a man by the name of D——, who kept a low tavern in a corner of the village, whose house was the resort of all the opposers of the revival. The barroom was a place of blasphemy; and he was himself a most profane, ungodly, abusive man. He went all over town mocking the revival and would take particular pains to swear and blaspheme whenever he saw a Christian.

Father Nash heard us speak of this Mr. D—— as "a hard case," and immediately he put his name upon his prayer list. He remained in town a day or two, and went on his way, having in view another area.

Not many days afterward, as we were holding an evening meeting with a very crowded house, who should come in but this notorious D——. His entrance created a considerable stir in the congregation. People feared that he had come in to make a disturbance. The fear and abhorrence of him had become very general among Christians, I believe, so that when he came in, some of the people got up and left. I knew his countenance, and kept my eyes upon him. I very soon became satisfied that he had not come in to oppose, and that he was under great conviction. He sat and writhed upon his seat and was very uneasy. He soon arose and trembling asked me if he might say a few words. I told him that he might. He then proceeded to make one of the most heartbroken confessions that I had ever heard. His confession seemed to cover the whole ground of his treatment of God, and of his treatment of Christians, and of the revival, and of everything good.

This thoroughly broke up the fallow ground in many hearts. It was the most powerful means that could have been used, just then, to give an impetus to the work. D—— soon came out and began to witness, abolished all the revelry and profanity of his barroom, and from that time, as long as I stayed there, and I know not how much longer, a prayer meeting was held in his barroom nearly every night.[2]

Question for Thought and Prayer

Do I need to attend God's school of prayer, or am I now able to pray in faith from a consecrated heart for the salvation of those who seem farthest from God?

---

[2]*Autobiography*, pp. 51-52, 70-72.

13

PRAYER FOR A NEW HEART

"Sinners are not converted by direct contact of the Holy Spirit, but by the truth, employed as a means. To expect the conversion of sinners by prayer alone, without the employment of truth, is to tempt God."[1]

The doctrines preached at Evans Mills were those which I always preached as the Gospel of Christ. I insisted upon the voluntary total moral depravity of the unregenerate, and the unalterable necessity of a radical change of heart by the Holy Ghost and by means of the truth.

I laid great stress upon prayer as an indispensable condition of promoting the revival. The atonement of Jesus Christ, His divinity, His divine mission, His perfect life, His vicarious death, His resurrection; and repentance, faith, justification by faith, and all kindred doctrines, were discussed as thoroughly as I was able, and pressed home, and were manifestly made efficacious by the power of the Holy Ghost.

The means used were simply preaching, prayer and conference meetings, much private prayer, much personal conversation, and meetings for the instruction of earnest inquirers. These and no other means were used for the promotion of the work.

I have spoken of the doctrines preached. I should add, that I always gave much instruction to inquirers. The prac-

---

[1]*Principles of Prayer*, p. 19.

tice had been, I believe, universal, to set anxious sinners to praying for a new heart, and to using means for their own conversion. The directions they received either assumed or implied that they were very willing to be Christians, and were taking much pain to persuade God to convert them. I tried to make them understand that God was using the means with them, and not they with Him; that God was willing, and they were unwilling; that God was ready, and they were not ready. In short, I tried to persuade them that present faith and repentance was the thing which God required of them, present and instant submission to His will, present and instant acceptance of Christ. I tried to show them that all delay was only an evasion of present duty; that all praying for a new heart was only trying to throw the responsibility of their own conversion upon God; and that all efforts to do duty while they did not give their hearts to God were hypocritical and delusive.[2]

Question for Thought and Prayer

Have you willingly given your heart to God in faith and repentance, or are your prayers still self-seeking and concerned about what you think God needs to do to your heart to save you?

---

[2]*Autobiography*, pp. 77, 79, 80.

14

PRAYER AND THE PULPIT

"Truth, by itself, will never produce the effect without the Spirit of God, and the Spirit is given in answer to prayer."[1]

My habit has always been to study the Gospel, and the best applications of it, all the time. I do not confine myself to hours and days of writing my sermons, but my mind is always pondering the truths of the Gospel and the best ways of using them. I go among the people and learn their wants. Then, in the light of the Holy Spirit, I take a subject that I think will meet their present situation and necessities. I think intensely on it, and pray much over the subject on Sabbath morning, for example, and get my mind full of it, and then go and pour it out to the people. Whereas, one great difficulty with a sermon is that a man after he has written it needs to think but little of the subject. He needs to pray but little. He perhaps reads over his manuscript Saturday evening, or Sabbath morning; but he does not feel the necessity of being powerfully anointed that his mouth may be opened and filled with arguments, and that he may be enabled to preach out a full heart. He is quite at ease. He has only to use his eyes and his voice, and he can preach in his way. It may be a sermon that has been written for years; it may be a sermon that he has written, every word of it, within the week. But on Sabbath day there is no freshness

---

[1]*Principles of Prayer*, p. 18.

in it. It does not come necessarily new and fresh, as an anointed message from God to his heart and through his heart to his people.

When I first began to preach, and for some twelve years of my earliest ministry, I wrote not a word; and was most commonly obliged to preach without any preparation whatsoever, except what I got in prayer. Oftentimes I went into the pulpit without knowing upon what text I should speak, or a word that I should say. I depended on the occasion and the Holy Spirit to suggest the text, and to open up the whole subject to my mind; and certainly in no part of my ministry have I preached with greater success and power. If I did not preach from inspiration, I don't know how I did preach. It was a common experience with me, and has been during all my ministerial life, that the subject would be opened up to my mind in a manner that was surprising to myself. It seemed that I could see with intuitive clearness just what I ought to say; and whole platoons of thoughts, words, and illustrations came to me as fast as I could deliver them. When I first began to make sermon outlines, I made them after and not before I preached. It was to preserve the outline of the thought which had been given me, on occasions such as I have just mentioned. I found when the Spirit of God had given me a very clear view of a subject, I could not retain it, to be used on any other occasion, unless I jotted down an outline of the thoughts. But after all, I have never found myself able to use old outlines in preaching, to any considerable extent, without rewriting them and having a fresh and new view of the subject given me by the Holy Spirit. I almost always get my subjects on my knees in prayer; and it has been a common experience with me, upon receiving a subject from the Holy Spirit, to have it make so strong an impression on my mind as to make me tremble, so that it was difficult to write. When subjects are thus given me that seem to go through me, body and soul, I can in a few moments make an outline that shall enable me to retain the view presented by the Spirit; and I find that such sermons always come with great power upon the people.

I am prepared to say, most solemnly, that I think I have studied all the more for not having written my sermons. I have been obliged to make the subjects upon which I preached familiar to my thoughts to fill my mind with them, and then go and talk them off to the people. I simply note the main points upon which I wish to dwell in the briefest possible manner, and in language not a word of which I use, perhaps, in preaching. I simply jot down the order of my propositions, and the propositions which I propose to take; and in a word, sketch an outline of the remarks and inferences with which I conclude.[2]

Question for Thought and Prayer

In how much of my Christian ministry and service to others do I rely more upon my thoughts and actions than upon prayer and the work of the Spirit of God?

---

[2]*Autobiography*, pp. 94-96.

15

PRAYER CONQUERS FEAR

"If you have the Spirit of God, you must expect to feel great distress in view of the condition of the church and of the world. . . . Read your Bibles and see how the prophets and apostles were always groaning and distressed in view of the state of the church and of the world."[1]

It was on Friday, if I remember right, that I arrived at Antwerp. (The people had no desire for public worship, and therefore the meetinghouse was locked up.) I called on some pious women and asked them if they would like to have a meeting. They said that they would, but they did not know that it would be possible. Mrs. —— agreed to open her parlor that evening for a meeting if I could get anybody to attend. I went about and invited the people, and secured the attendance, I think, of some thirteen in her parlor. I preached to them and then said that if I could get the use of the village schoolhouse, I would preach on Sabbath. I got the consent of the trustees, and the next day an appointment was circulated around among the people for a meeting at the schoolhouse Sabbath morning.

In passing around the village I heard a vast amount of profanity. I thought I had never heard so much in any place I ever visited. It seemed as if the men, in playing ball upon the green, and in every business place that I stepped into, were all cursing and swearing and damning each other. I

---

[1]*Principles of Prayer*, pp. 82, 83.

felt as if I had arrived upon the borders of hell. I had a kind of awful feeling, I recollect, as I passed around the village on Saturday. The very atmosphere seemed to me to be poison, and a kind of terror took possession of me.

I gave myself to prayer on Saturday and finally urged my petition till this answer came: "Be not afraid, but speak, and hold not thy peace; for I am with thee, and no man shall set on thee to hurt thee. For I have much people in this city." This completely relieved me of all fear. I found, however, that the Christian people there were really afraid that something serious might happen if religious meetings were again established in that place. I spent Saturday very much in prayer, but passed around the village enough to see that the appointment that had been given out for preaching at the schoolhouse was making quite an excitement.

Sabbath morning I arose and left my lodgings in the hotel; and in order to get alone, where I could let out my voice as well as my heart, I went up into the woods at some distance from the village and continued for a long time in prayer. However, I did not get relief, and went up a second time, but the load upon my mind increased, and I did not find relief. I went up a third time, and then the answer came. I found that it was time for meeting, and I went immediately to the schoolhouse. I found it packed to its utmost capacity. I had my pocket Bible in my hand, and read to them this text: "God so loved the world, that he gave his only begotten Son, that whosoever believeth in him should not perish, but have everlasting life." I cannot remember much that I said, but I know that the point on which my mind principally labored was the treatment which God received in return for His love. The subject affected my own mind very much, and I preached and poured out my soul and my tears together.

I saw several of the men there from whom I had, the day before, heard the most awful profanity. I pointed them out in the meeting and told what they had said—how they had called on God to damn each other. Indeed, I let loose my whole heart upon them. I told them they seemed "to howl blasphemy about the streets like hell-hounds"; and it seemed to me that I had arrived "on the very verge of hell." Everybody knew that what I said was true. They cowered under it. They did not appear offended, but the people wept about as much as I did myself. I think there were scarcely any dry eyes in the house.

Mr. C—— had refused to open the meetinghouse in the morning. But as soon as these first services closed, he arose and said to the people that he would open the meetinghouse in the afternoon.

The people scattered, and carried the information in every direction; and in the afternoon the meetinghouse was almost as crowded as the schoolhouse had been in the morning. Everybody was out at meeting; and the Lord let me loose upon them in a convicting manner.[2]

Question for Thought and Prayer

Do I often not speak out because I am afraid of people and of what they might say and do, or do I consistently pray for the Spirit of God to give me courage and a promise from Scripture?

---

[2]*Autobiography*, pp. 99, 100.

16

PRAYER AND REVIVAL

"Strong desires vividly illustrate the strength of God's feelings. They are like the real feelings of God for impenitent sinners. When I have seen, as I sometimes have, the amazing strength of love for souls that has been felt by Christians, I have been wonderfully impressed with the amazing love of God and His desire for their salvation."[1]

I have said that the spirit of prayer that prevailed in revivals was a very marked feature of them. It was common for young converts to be greatly burdened in prayer; and thus in some instances, so much so, that they were constrained to pray whole nights, and until their bodily strength was quite exhausted, for the conversion of souls around them. There was a great pressure of the Holy Spirit upon the minds of Christians; and they seemed to bear about with them the burden of immortal souls. They manifested the greatest solemnity of mind and the greatest watchfulness in all their words and actions. It was very common to find Christians, whenever they met in any place, instead of engaging in conversation, to fall on their knees in prayer.

Not only were prayer meetings greatly multiplied and fully attended, not only was there great solemnity in those meetings; but there was a mighty spirit of secret prayer. Christians prayed a great deal, many of them spending

---

[1]*Principles of Prayer*, p. 36.

many hours in private prayer. It was also the case that two or more would take the promise: "If two of you shall agree on earth as touching anything that they shall ask, it shall be done for them of my Father which is in heaven," and make some particular person a subject of prayer; and it was wonderful to what an extent they prevailed. Answers to prayer were so manifestly multiplied on every side that no one could escape the conviction that God was daily and hourly answering prayer.

If anything occurred that threatened to mar the work, if there was any appearance of any root of bitterness springing up, or any tendency to fanaticism or disorder, Christians would take the alarm and give themselves to prayer that God would direct and control all things. And it was surprising to see to what extent and by what means God would remove obstacles out of the way in answer to prayer.

In regard to my own experience, I will say that unless I had the spirit of prayer I could do nothing. If even for a day or an hour I lost the spirit of grace and supplication, I found myself unable to preach with power and efficiency, or to win souls by personal conversation. In this respect my experience was what it has always been. [I found myself having more or less power in preaching, and in personal labors for souls, just in proportion as I had the spirit of prevailing prayer. I have found that unless I kept myself and have been kept in such relations to God as to have daily and hourly access to Him in prayer, my efforts to win souls were abortive; but that when I could prevail with God in prayer, I could prevail with man in preaching, exhortation, and conversation.]

[I have stated that my last field of labor in St. Lawrence County was in De Kalb, and that the revival there was powerful for the scattered populations that then existed in that new region of country.] For several weeks before I left De Kalb to go to the synod [in Oneida County of which I have made mention], I was very strongly exercised in prayer, and had an experience that was somewhat new to me. I found myself so much exercised, and so borne down with the weight of immortal souls, that I was constrained to pray without ceasing. [I could not rest in the house and was obliged to retire to the barn frequently through the day, where I would unburden my soul and pour out my heart to God in prayer. I had wonderful faith given to me at that time, and had some experiences that alarmed me. When alone I would wrestle and struggle, and my faith would rise till I would say to God] that He had made a promise to answer prayer, and I could not, and would not, be denied. [I could be so burdened as to use such strong language to God in prayer.] I felt so certain that He would hear me, and that faithfulness to His promises, and to himself, rendered it impossible that He should not hear and answer, that frequently I found myself saying to Him, "I hope Thou dost not think that I can be denied. I come with Thy faithful promises in my hand, and I cannot be denied."

[At that time the Spirit of God made such application of the promises to my mind, and so revealed their real meaning, as to lead me to understand better how to use them, and to what cases they were specially applicable, than I had ever understood before. I had been in the habit from my first conversion of having the Spirit in prayer lead me to such application of the promises, as I never should have gotten by any study of my own. I had also come to realize that these promises had a much wider application in their spirit than a mere critical examination of their letter would have warranted. I was led frequently to see that the New Testament writers quoted the promises of the Old Testament in such a way as to cover much more ground than the mere letter of the promises would have warranted. But this experience of mine at De Kalb was extraordinary in this respect.][2]

---

[2]See Appendix A for G. F. Wright's comments on Finney's prayer of faith.

I cannot tell how absurd unbelief looked to me, and how certain it was, in my mind, that God would answer prayer—those prayers that, from day to day and from hour to hour, I found myself offering in such agony and faith. I had no idea of the shape the answer would take, the locality in which the prayers would be answered, or the exact time of the answer. My impression was that the answer was near, even at the door; and I felt myself strengthened in the divine life, put on the harness for a mighty conflict with the powers of darkness, and expected soon to see a far more powerful outpouring of the Spirit of God in that new country where I had been laboring.[3]

Question for Thought and Prayer

Have I so studied God's Word, and am I so open to the Holy Spirit's guidance, that I can see who and what I am to pray for and so I can apply the promises of Scripture to the needs I perceive?

---

[3]*Autobiography*, pp. 141-143.

17

FAMILY PRAYER

"True Christianity does not consist in obeying our feelings, but in conforming our heart to perceived biblical truth. God has given us reason, and requires us to understand what we are about."[1]

I remember the situation of a young woman at Western, in a distant part of the town, who came to the meeting at the center almost every day. I had conversed with her several times and found her deeply convicted, and indeed, almost in despair. I was expecting to hear, from day to day, that she had been converted; but she remained unchanged, except her despair increased. This led me to suspect that something was wrong at home. I asked her if her parents were Christians. She said they were members of the church. I asked her if they attended meetings. She said, "Yes, on the Sabbath." "Do not your parents attend meetings at other times?" "No," was the reply. "Do you have family prayers at home?" "No, sir," she said. "We used to have; but we have not had family prayers for a long time." This revealed the problem to me at once. I inquired when I could possibly find her father and mother at home. She said, almost any time, as they were seldom away from home. Feeling that it was infinitely dangerous to leave this case as it was, I went the next morning to see the family.

---

[1]*Principles of Prayer*, p. 95.

This daughter was, I think, an only child; at any rate, she was the only child at home. I found her dejected and sunken in despair. I said to her mother, "The Spirit of the Lord is striving with your daughter." "Yes," she said, "I don't know but that He is." I asked her if she was praying for her. She gave me an answer that led me to understand that she did not know what it was to pray for her. I inquired for her husband. She said that he was in the field at work. I asked her to call him in. He came, and as he came in I said to him, "Do you see the state that your daughter is in?" He replied that he thought she felt very bad. "And are you concerned and praying for her?" His answer revealed the fact that if he was ever converted, he was a miserable backslider and had no hold upon God whatever. "And," said I, "you do not have family prayers." "No, sir." "Now," said I, "I have seen your daughter, day after day, bowed down with conviction, and I have learned that the difficulty is here at home. You have shut up the kingdom of heaven against your daughter. You neither enter yourself, nor will you suffer her to enter. Your unbelief and worldly-mindedness prevent the conversion of your daughter, and will ruin your own soul. Now you must repent. I do not intend to leave this house until you and your wife repent and get out of the way of your daughter. You must establish family prayer and build up the altar that has fallen down. Now, my dear sir, will you get down here on your knees, you and your wife, and engage in prayer? And will you promise that from this time you will do your duty, set up your family altar, and return to God?"

I was so earnest with them that they both began to weep. My faith was so strong that I did not trifle when I told them that I would not leave the house until they would repent and establish their family altar. I felt that the work must be done, and done then. I cast myself down upon my knees and began to pray, and they knelt down and wept sorely. I confessed for them as well as I could, and tried to lead them to God, and to prevail with God in their behalf. It was a moving scene. They both humbled themselves and confessed their sins, and before we rose from our knees the daughter was manifestly converted. She arose rejoicing in Christ. Many answers to prayer and many scenes of great interest were presented in this revival.[2]

Question for Thought and Prayer

Is there any stumbling block in your life and in the life of your family that is influencing someone to resist God's call?

---

[2]*Autobiography*, pp. 151, 152.

18

PRAYER AND FAITH

*"You must pray in faith. You must expect to obtain the
things for which you ask. Do not look for an answer to
prayer if you pray without any expectation of obtaining it.
You are not to form such expectations without any reason
for them. In the cases I have supposed, there is a reason for
the expectation."*[1]

I should say a few words in regard to the kind of prayer
which prevailed at Rome at this time. I think it was on the
Saturday that I came down from Western to exchange with
Mr. Gillett that I met the church people in the afternoon in
a prayer meeting in their house of worship. I endeavored to
make them understand that God would immediately answer prayer, provided they fulfilled the conditions upon
which He had promised to answer prayer, and especially if
they believed in the sense of expecting Him to answer their
requests. I observed that they were greatly interested in my
remarks, and their countenance manifested an intense desire to see an answer to their prayers. Near the close of the
meeting I recollect making this remark: "I really believe, if
you will unite this afternoon in the prayer of faith to God for
the immediate outpouring of His Spirit, you will receive an
answer from heaven sooner than you would get a message
from Albany by the quickest mail service that could be
sent."

---

[1]*Principles of Prayer*, p. 34.

I said this with great emphasis, and felt it; and I observed that the people were startled with my expression of earnestness and faith in respect to an immediate answer to prayer. The fact is, I had so often seen this result in answer to prayer that I made the remark without any misgiving. Nothing was said by any of the members of the church at the time, but I learned after the work had begun that three or four members of the church called at Mr. Gillett's study, and felt so impressed with what had been said about speedy answers to prayer that they determined to take God at His word and see whether He would answer while they were yet speaking. One of them told me afterward that they had wonderful faith given them by the Spirit of God to pray for an immediate answer, and he added, "The answer did come quicker than we could have gotten an answer from Albany by the quickest mail service that could have been sent."

Indeed the town was full of prayer. Go where you would, you heard the voice of prayer. Pass along the street, and if two or three Christians happened to be together, they were praying. Wherever they met they prayed. Wherever there was a sinner unconverted, especially if he manifested any opposition, you would find some two or three brethren or sisters agreeing to make him a particular subject of prayer; [and it was very remarkable to see to what an extent God would answer prayer immediately].[2]

Question for Thought and Prayer

Is your relationship with God so developed that you can know what things to pray for in faith, knowing that to encourage others in specific prayers will increase their faith?

---

[2]*Autobiography*, pp. 171, 172.

19

PRAYER AND OPPOSITION

*"If you have much of the Spirit of God, you must make
up your mind to have much opposition, both in the church
and in the world. Very likely the leading men in the church
will oppose you. So it was when Christ was on earth. . . . If
you are filled with the Spirit, you will not find yourselves
distressed, and galled, and worried when people speak
against you."*[1]

I must return to what happened at Auburn. I became,
soon after I went there, very much impressed with the extensive working of that system of espionage of which I have
spoken.[2] Mr. Frost, of Whitesboro, had come to a knowledge of the facts to a considerable extent, and related them
to me. I said nothing publicly, or as I recollect, privately, to
anybody on the subject; but gave myself to prayer. I looked
to God with great earnestness day after day to be directed,
asking Him to show me the path of duty and to give me
grace to ride out the storm.

I shall never forget what a scene I passed through one
day in my room at Dr. Lansing's [in Auburn, soon after my
arrival there]. The Lord showed me as in a vision what [I
had to pass through]. He drew so near to me during prayer
that my flesh literally trembled on my bones. I shook from

---

[1]*Principles of Prayer*, pp. 84, 89.
[2]See the *Autobiography* for the complete details of this event.

head to foot [like a man in an epileptic seizure] under a full sense of the presence of God. At first, and for some time, it seemed more like being on the top of Sinai, amidst its full thunderings, than in the presence of the cross of Christ.

Never in my life, that I recollect, was I so awed and humbled before God as then. Nevertheless, instead of feeling like fleeing, I seemed drawn nearer and nearer to that Presence that filled me with such unutterable awe and trembling. After a season of great humiliation before Him, there came a great lifting up. God assured me that He would be with me and uphold me; that no opposition should prevail against me; that I had nothing to do, in regard to all this matter, but to keep about my work and wait for the salvation of God.

The sense of God's presence, and all that passed between God and my soul at that time, I can never describe. It led me to be perfectly trustful, perfectly calm, and to have nothing but the most perfectly kind feelings toward all the brethren that were misled and were arraying themselves against me. I felt assured that all would come out right, that my true course was to leave everything to God and to keep about my work. And as the storm gathered and the opposition increased, I never for one moment doubted how it would result. I was never disturbed by it, I never spent a waking hour in thinking of it, when to all outward appearance, it seemed as if all the churches of the land, except where I had labored, would unite to shut me out of their pulpits. This was indeed the avowed determination, as I understood, of the men who led in the opposition. They were so deceived that they thought there was no effectual way but to unite, and, as they expressed it, "put him down." But God assured me that they could not put me down.[3]

---

[3]*Autobiography*, pp. 193-194.

Question for Thought and Prayer

Can I pray to God in the midst of opposition to my work for Him, and do so with perfectly kind feelings toward those who are against me?

20

PRAYER OVERCOMES IGNORANCE

"There are many who believe in the existence of God but do not believe in the efficacy of prayer. They profess to believe in God but deny the necessity or influence of prayer."[1]

In the spring of 1829, when the Delaware River was high, the lumbermen came down with their rafts from the region of the high land, where they had been getting the lumber out during the winter. At that time there was a large tract of country along the northern region of Pennsylvania, called by many "the lumber region," that extended up toward the head waters of the Delaware River.

Many of the lumbermen were raising families in that region, and there was a large tract of country unsettled and unoccupied, except by these lumbermen. They had no schools and, at that time, no churches or religious privileges at all. I knew a minister who told me he was born in that lumber region, and that when he was twenty years old, he had never attended a religious meeting and did not know his alphabet.

These men that came down with lumber attended our meetings, and quite a number of them were hopefully converted. They went back into the wilderness and began to pray for the outpouring of the Holy Spirit and to tell the people around them what they had seen in Philadelphia, exhorting them to attend to their salvation. Their efforts

---

[1]*Principles of Prayer*, p. 44.

were immediately blessed, and the revival began to take hold and to spread among those lumbermen. It went on in a most powerful and remarkable manner. It spread to such an extent that in many cases persons would be convicted and converted, who had not attended any meetings, and who were almost as ignorant as heathen. Men who were getting out lumber, and were living in little shanties alone, or where two or three or more were together, would be seized with such conviction that it would lead them to wander off and inquire what they should do. They would be converted, and thus the revival spread. There was the greatest simplicity manifested by the converts.

An aged minister who had been somewhat acquainted with the circumstances, related to me as an example of what was going on there the following fact. He said one man in a certain place had a little shanty by himself where he slept nights. He began to feel that he was a sinner, and his convictions increased upon him until he broke down, confessed his sins, and repented; and the Spirit of God revealed to him so much of the way of salvation that he evidently knew the Savior. But he had never attended a prayer meeting, or heard a prayer, that he recollected, in his life. His feelings became such that he finally felt constrained to go and tell some of his acquaintances how he felt. But when he arrived, he found that they felt, a good many of them, just as he did, and that they were holding prayer meetings. He attended their prayer meetings and heard them pray, and finally prayed himself; and this was the form of his prayer: "Lord, you have got me down and I hope you will keep me down. And since you have had such good luck with me, I hope you will try other sinners."

I have said that this work began in the spring of 1829, as the result of a few men having attended some of our meetings. In the spring of 1831, I was at Auburn again. Two or three men from this lumber region came to see me and to inquire how they could get some ministers to go in there.

They said that not less than five thousand people had been converted in that lumber region; that the revival had extended itself along for eighty miles, and there was not a single minister of the gospel there.[2]

I have never been in that region; but from all I have ever heard about it, I have regarded that as one of the most remarkable revivals that have occurred in this country. It was carried on almost independently of the ministry, among a class of people very ignorant in regard to all ordinary instruction; and yet so clear and wonderful were the teachings of God that I have always understood the revival was remarkably free from fanaticism, or wildness, or anything that was objectionable. "Behold how great a matter a little fire kindleth!" The spark that was struck into the hearts of those few lumbermen that came to Philadelphia spread over that forest and resulted in the salvation of a multitude of souls.[3]

Questions for Thought and Prayer

Do I really understand how important my prayers and my witnessing are? The effort I expend today may lead thousands in other lands, or even yet unborn, to find the Savior. Am I willing to expend that effort for the cause of God's Kingdom?

---

[2]Let the reader not forget, however, that it was the preaching of Finney and the praying of Finney and others that motivated those few men to return with the Gospel to their brothers in that region.

[3]*Autobiography*, pp. 250-252. Finney, in his humility, does not underscore the great impact of the truth he preached upon the minds of those who declared that same truth to others in that region.

21

PRAYER AND DIFFICULT DECISIONS

"There are three ways in which God's will is revealed to men for their guidance in prayer: by express promises or predictions in the Bible; by His Providence; and by His Spirit."[1]

Leaving New York I spent a few weeks in Whitestown, and as was common, being pressed to go in many directions, I was greatly at a loss as to what my duty was. But among others, an urgent invitation was received from the Third Presbyterian Church in Rochester, of which Mr. Parker had been pastor, to go there and supply them for a period of time.

I inquired into the circumstances and found that on several accounts it was a very unpromising field of labor.[2]

With many pressing invitations before me, I felt as I have often felt, greatly perplexed. I remained at my father-in-law's and considered the subject until I felt that I must take hold and work somewhere. Accordingly we packed our trunks and went down to Utica, about seven miles distant, where I had many praying friends. We arrived there in the afternoon; and in the evening quite a number of the leading brethren, in whose prayers and wisdom I had a great deal of

---

[1]*Principles of Prayer*, p. 22.

[2]For details of the circumstances, see the *Autobiography*. Finney was always courageous in the Spirit, and did not flee difficult situations.

confidence, at my request met for consultation and prayer in regard to my next field of labor. I laid all the facts before them in regard to Rochester. And insofar as I was acquainted with them, the leading facts in respect to the other places to which I was invited at that time. Rochester seemed to be the least inviting of them all.

After talking the matter over and having several seasons of prayer, interspersed with conversation, the brethren gave their opinions one after another, in relation to what they thought it wise for me to do. They were unanimous in the opinion that Rochester was too uninviting a place of labor to be put at all in competition with New York, or Philadelphia, or some other places to which I was then invited. They were firm in the conviction that I should go east from Utica, not west. At the time, this was my own impression and conviction, and I retired from this meeting, as I supposed, settled not to go to Rochester, but to New York or Philadelphia. This was before railroads existed, and when we parted that evening I expected to take the canal boat, which was the most convenient way for a family to travel, and start in the morning for New York.

But after I retired to my lodging the question was presented to my mind under a different aspect. Something seemed to question me: "What are the reasons that deter you from going to Rochester?" I could readily enumerate them, but then the question returned: "Ah! but are these good reasons? Certainly you are needed at Rochester all the more because of these difficulties. Do you shun the place because there are so many things that need to be corrected, because there is so much that is wrong? But if all was right, you would not be needed." I soon came to the conclusion that we were all wrong, and that the reasons that had determined us against my going to Rochester were the most cogent reasons for my going. I felt ashamed to shrink from undertaking the work because of its difficulties, and it was strongly impressed upon me that the Lord would be with me and that that was my field. My mind became entirely decided before I retired to rest that Rochester was the place to which the Lord would have me go. I informed my wife of my decision; and accordingly, early in the morning, before the people were generally moving in the city, the packet boat came along, and we embarked and went westward instead of eastward.

The brethren in Utica were greatly surprised when they learned of this change in our destination, and awaited the result with a good deal of anxiety.[3]

Question for Thought and Prayer

Do I have a tendency to pray for and expect God to grant me the most pleasing labors in His Kingdom?

---

[3]*Autobiography*, pp. 284-286. See the following pages in his *Autobiography* for the amazing revival that occurred in Rochester.

22

PRAYER AND CONVERSION

"Prevailing, or effectual, prayer is that prayer which attains the blessing that it seeks."[1]

Soon, there were very marked conversions in Rochester. The wife of a prominent lawyer in that city was one of the first converts. She was a woman of high standing, a lady of culture and extensive influence. Her conversion was a very marked one. The first time I saw her, a friend of hers came with her to my room and introduced her. The lady who introduced her was a Christian, who had found that her friend was under great conviction, and persuaded her to come to see me.

Mrs. M—— had been an intelligent, worldly woman and very fond of society's ways. She afterward told me that when I first came there, she greatly regretted it, and feared there would be a revival. She believed a revival would greatly interfere with the pleasures and amusements that she had promised herself that winter. On conversing with her I found that the Spirit of the Lord was indeed dealing with her, in an unsparing manner. She was deeply burdened with great conviction of sin. After considerable conversation with her, I pressed her earnestly to renounce sin, and the world, and self, and everything for Christ. I saw

---

[1]*Principles of Prayer*, p. 17.

that she was a very proud woman, and this struck me as rather the most marked feature of her character. At the conclusion of our conversation, we knelt down to pray; and my mind being full of the subject of the pride of her heart, as it was manifested, I very soon introduced the text: "Except ye be converted and become as little children, ye shall in no wise enter into the kingdom of heaven." [Thus I seemed to be led by the Spirit of prayer, almost irresistibly.] I turned this subject over in prayer; and almost immediately I heard Mrs. M——, as she was kneeling by my side, repeating that text: "Except ye be converted and become as little children—as little children—Except ye be converted and become as little children." I observed that her mind was taken with that, and the Spirit of God was pressing it upon her heart. I therefore continued to pray, holding that subject before her mind, and holding her up before God as needing that very thing to be converted—to become as a little child. [I besought the Lord to convert her, to make her as a little child, to put away her pride and her loftiness of spirit and bring her down into the attitude of a little child.]

I felt that the Lord was answering prayer. I felt sure that He was doing the very work I asked Him to do. Her pride broke, her confession gushed forth, and before we rose from our knees, she was indeed a little child. When I stopped praying and opened my eyes and looked at her, her face was turned up toward heaven, and the tears streaming down; and she was in the attitude of praying that she might be made a little child. She rose up, became peaceful, settled into a joyous faith, and retired. From that moment she was outspoken in her convictions, and zealous for the conversion of her friends. Her conversion, of course, produced much excitement among that class of people to which she belonged.[2]

---

[2]*Autobiography*, pp. 287, 288.

Question for Thought and Prayer

Is my pride, or my desire to be looked up to, standing in the way of prevailing with God in prayer; or do I need to be humbled by Him in order to be heard by Him?

23

AUTHORITY OF SCRIPTURE

"Aim to obey perfectly the written law. In other words, have no fellowship with sin. If you sin at all, let it be your daily grief. The man who does not aim at this, means to live in sin. Such a man need not expect God's blessing, for he is not sincere in desiring to keep all His commandments."[1]

Among other conversions in Rochester, I must not forget to mention that of Mr. P——, a prominent citizen of that place, a bookseller. Mr. P—— was an infidel; not an atheist, but a disbeliever in the divine authority of the Bible. He was a reader and a thinker, a man of keen, shrewd mind, strong will, and most decided character. He was, I believe, a man of good outward morals and a gentleman highly respected. He came to my room early one morning and said to me, "Mr. Finney, there is a great movement here on the subject of Christianity, but I am a skeptic, and I want you to prove to me that the Bible is true." The Lord enabled me at once to discern his state of mind, so far as to decide the course I should take with him. I said to him, "Do you believe in the existence of God?" "Oh, yes!" he said. "I am not an atheist." "Well, do you believe that you have treated God as you ought? Have you respected His authority? Have you loved Him? Have you done that which you thought would please Him, and with the design to please Him?

---

[1]*Principles of Prayer*, p. 73.

Don't you admit that you ought to love Him, and ought to worship Him, and ought to obey Him according to the best light you have?" "Oh, yes!" he said. "I admit all this." "But have you done so?" I asked. "Why no," he answered, "I cannot say that I have." "Well then," I replied, "why should I give you further information, and further light, if you will not do your duty and obey the light you already have? Now," I said, "when you will make up your mind to live up to your convictions, to obey God according to the best light you have; when you will make up your mind to repent of your neglect thus far, and to please God just as well as you know how, the rest of your life, I will try to show you that the Bible is from God. Until then it is of no use for me to do any such thing."[2] I did not sit down, and I think had not asked him to sit down. He replied, "That is fair," and retired.

I heard no more of him until the next morning. Soon after I arose, he came to my room again; and as soon as he entered, he clapped his hands and said, "Mr. Finney, God has wrought a miracle! I went down to the store," he continued, "after I left your room, thinking of what you had said; and I made up my mind that I would repent of what I knew was wrong in my relations to God, and that hereafter I would live according to the best light I had. And when I made up my mind to do this," said he, "my feelings so overcame me that I fell; and I do not know but I should have died if it had not been for Mr.——, who was with me in the store." From this time he has been, as all who know him are aware, a praying, earnest Christian man. For many years he has been one of the trustees of Oberlin College, has stood by us through all our trials, and has aided us with his means and his whole influence.[3]

---

[2]For a detailed argument by Charles Finney on the Authority of Scripture, see his, *The Heart of Truth*, pp. 39-57.

[3]*Autobiography*, pp. 298, 299.

Question for Thought and Prayer

Have I sold out my all to the Lord Jesus Christ, resolving to be obedient in all things according to His Word?

24

PRAYING IN THE HOLY SPIRIT

*"Many Christians are so ignorant of the Spirit's influ-
ences, and have thought so little about having His assis-
tance in prayer, that when they have such influences they
do not know it, and so do not yield to them, and cherish
them. We are sensing nothing in the case—only the movement of our own minds. There is nothing else that can be
felt. We are merely sensing that our thoughts are intensely
employed on a certain subject."*[1]

In the morning, after sleeping quietly at Mr. S——'s in
Auburn, I had arisen and was preparing to take the stage,
which was to arrive in the early part of the day, when a
gentleman came in with the request for me to remain—a request in writing, signed by a large number of influential
men who had opposed my efforts at revival in 1826 in their
city. These men had set themselves against the revival
then, and had broken from their church. The request in
writing was an earnest appeal to me to stop and labor for
their salvation, and it was signed by a long list of unconverted men. I was utterly amazed. In this paper they allud-
ed to the opposition they had formerly made to my labors,
and besought me to overlook it, and stop and preach the
Gospel to them.

I went to my room, and spread the matter before God,
and soon made up my mind what to do. I told the pastor

---

[1]*Principles of Prayer*, p. 68.

and his elders that I was nearly exhausted, but that upon certain conditions I would remain. I would preach twice on Sunday and two evenings during the week, but I asked that they should take all the other responsibilities upon themselves. They must not expect me to attend any meetings other than those at which I preached; they must counsel those that come forward; and they must conduct the prayer and the other meetings. I knew that they understood how to deal with sinners, and could well trust them to perform that part of the work.

The word took immediate effect. On the first or second Sunday evening that I preached, I saw that the Word was taking such powerful hold that at the close I called for those whose minds were made up, to come forward, publicly renounce their sins, and give themselves to Christ.[2] Much to my own surprise, and very much to the surprise of the pastor and many members of the church, the first man I observed coming forward and leading the way was the man who had led, and exerted more influence than any other man, in the opposition to the former revival. He came forward promptly, followed by a large number of the persons who had signed that paper; and that evening there was such a demonstration made as to produce a general interest throughout the place.

I have spoken of Mr. Clary as the praying man who was at Rochester.[3] He had a brother, a physician, living in Auburn. I think it was the second Sunday I was at Auburn at this time that I observed in the congregation the solemn face of this Mr. Clary. He looked as if he was weighed down with an agony of prayer. Being well acquainted with him, and knowing the great gift of God that was upon him, the spirit of prayer, I was very glad to see him there. He sat in the pew with his brother, the doctor, who was "religious"

---

[2]For an excellent description by Charles Finney of the reasons for asking sinners to come forward, see *Principles of Liberty*, p. 17.

[3]*Autobiography*, pp. 296, 297.

but who knew nothing by experience, I should think, of his brother Abel's great power with God.

After worship we went to the doctor's house for some refreshments. We gathered about the table, and Dr. Clary turned to his brother and said, "Brother Abel, will you ask a blessing?" Brother Abel bowed his head and began, audibly, to ask a blessing. He had uttered but a sentence or two when he broke instantly down, moved suddenly back from the table, and fled to his chamber. The doctor supposed he had been taken suddenly ill, and rose up and followed him. In a few moments he came down and said, "Mr. Finney, brother Abel wants to see you." I asked, "What's wrong?" He replied, "I do not know; but he says you know." He appears to be in great distress, but I think it is conviction." I understood it in a moment and went to his room. He lay groaning upon the bed, the Spirit making intercession for him, and in him, with groanings that could not be uttered. I had barely entered the room when he made out to say, "Pray, brother Finney." I knelt down and helped him in prayer by directing his prayers for the conversion of sinners. I continued to pray until his distress passed away, and then I returned to the dinner table.

I understood that this was the voice of God. I saw the Spirit of prayer was upon him, and I felt his influence upon myself, and took it for granted that the work would move on more powerfully. It did so. I believe, but am not quite sure, that every one of those men who signed that paper, making a long list of names, was converted during that revival.[4]

Questions for Thought and Prayer

Are you willing to labor so in prayer for the conversion of souls, even for those whom you do not know, that you would be in great agony of spirit? Or do you prefer to pray that way only for yourself?"

---

[4]*Autobiography*, pp. 303-306.

25

REVIVAL LECTURES AND PRAYER

"The Christian has natural power to pray, and so far as the will of God is revealed, is able to do it; but he never does unless the Spirit of God influences him. . . . The Holy Spirit helps Christians to pray "according to the will of God," or for the things that God desires them to pray for."[1]

In January 1834, I was obliged to leave New York on account of my health, and take a sea voyage. I went up the Mediterranean, therefore, in a small brig, in the midst of winter. We had a very stormy passage. My stateroom was small, and I was on the whole, very uncomfortable; and the voyage did not much improve my health. I spent some weeks at Malta, and also in Sicily. I was gone about six months.

On my homeward passage my mind became exceedingly exercised on the question of revivals. I feared that they would decline throughout the country. I feared that the opposition that had been made to them had grieved the Holy Spirit. My own health, it appeared to me, had nearly or quite broken down; and I knew of no other evangelist that would take the field and aid pastors in revival work. This view of the subject distressed me so much that one day I found myself unable to rest. My soul was in an utter agony. I spent almost the entire day in prayer [there on my knees]

---

[1]*Principles of Prayer*, pp. 59, 60.

in my stateroom, or walking the deck in [such pain as to wring my hands and almost gnaw my tongue, as it were, for pain and agony] in view of the state of things. In fact, I felt crushed with the burden that was on my soul. There was no one on board to whom I could open my mind or say a word.

It was the spirit of prayer that was upon me; that which I had often before experienced in kind but perhaps never before to such a degree, for so long a time. I besought the Lord to go on with His work and to provide himself with such instruments as were necessary. It was a long summer day in the early part of July. After a day of unspeakable wrestling and agony in my soul, just at night, the subject was clarified to my mind. The Spirit led me to believe that all would come out right, and that God had yet a work for me to do; that I might be at rest; that the Lord would go forward with His work and give me strength to take any part in it that He desired. But I had not the least idea what the course of His providence would be.

(Finney continues in his account to explain why he was commissioned to preach a series of Lectures on Revival for his New York congregation and for publication in the *New York Evangelist*. These lectures contain most of his principles of prayer. He then proceeds with his account of God's blessing on these lectures. The full account of the circumstances can be found in *Principles of Prayer*, pp. 107-111.)

These lectures were afterward published in a book, and called, *Finney's Lectures on Revivals*. Twelve thousand copies were sold, as fast as they could be printed. And here, for the glory of Christ, I would say, that they have been reprinted in England and France. They were translated into Welsh; and on the Continent were translated into French and, I believe, into German; and were very extensively circulated throughout Europe and the colonies of Great Britain. They were, I presume, to be found wherever the English language is spoken. After they had been printed in Welsh, the Congregational ministers of the Principality of

Wales, at one of their public meetings, appointed a committee to inform me of the great revival that had resulted from the translation of those lectures into the Welsh language. This they did by letter. One publisher in London informed me that his father had published eighty thousand volumes of them. [I do not know into how many languages they have been translated. But I mention this particularly as being an answer to prayer.] These revival lectures, meager as was the report of them, and feeble as they were in themselves, have been instrumental, as I have learned, in promoting revivals in England, and Scotland, and Wales, on the Continent in various places, in Canada, east and west, in Nova Scotia, and in some of the islands of the sea.

In England and Scotland, I have often been encouraged by meeting with ministers and laymen, in great numbers, that had been converted, directly or indirectly, through the instrumentality of those lectures. I recollect the last time that I was abroad, one evening, three very prominent ministers of the Gospel introduced themselves to me, after the sermon, and said that when they were in college they got hold of my revival lectures, which had resulted in their becoming ministers. I found persons in England, in all the different denominations, who had not only read those revival lectures, but had been greatly blessed in reading them. When they were first published in the *New York Evangelist*, the reading of them resulted in revivals of religion in multitudes of places throughout the country.

But this was not of man's wisdom. Let the reader remember that long day of agony and prayer at sea, that God would do something to forward the work of revivals, and enable me, if He desired to do it, to take such a course as to help forward the work. I felt certain then that my prayers would be answered; and I have regarded all that I have since been able to accomplish, [and all the results of preaching and publishing those lectures, as well as all else that I have been in any wise instrumental in accomplishing

for the Zion of God, is in a very important sense an answer
to the prayers of that day. It has always been my experience
that when I have a day or season of great travail of soul for
any object, if I pursue the subject, and continue my pleadings until I prevail and my soul is at rest, that in answer to
such prayers God not only gives me what I ask, but exceedingly above all that I at the time had in my mind. God has
been answering the prayers of that day on shipboard for
more than thirty years.[2]

Nobody but myself can appreciate the wonderful manner in which those agonizing throes of my soul on that occasion have met with the divine response. Indeed, it was God,
the Holy Ghost, asking intercession in me. The prayer was
not properly mine, but the prayer of the Holy Spirit. It was
no righteousness or worthiness of my own at all.][3] The spirit
of prayer came upon me as a sovereign grace, bestowed
upon me without the least merit and despite all of my sin-
fulness. He pressed my soul in prayer until I was enabled to
prevail; and through the infinite riches of grace in Christ
Jesus, I have been many years witnessing the wonderful results of that day of wrestling with God. In answer to that
day's agony He has continued to give me the spirit of
prayer.[4]

---

[2]I believe that God is even now answering the prayers that Finney offered so long ago. There is still much interest in and study of
his principles of prayer and revival. Jonathan Goforth says of Finney's influence upon him and the revivals in China: "Selections
from *Finney's Autobiography and Revival Lectures* were sent to
me by a friend in India (the fall of 1905). It was the final something
which set me on fire. . . . 'If Finney is right,' I vowed, 'then I'm going to find out what those laws are and obey them, no matter what
it costs.' " *"By My Spirit"* by Jonathan Goforth (Minneapolis:
Bethany Fellowship, 1964), pp. 19, 20.

[3]Of course, Finney would not have denied that his own agency
was important in responding to the leading of the Spirit of God.
These words express his humility and praise for the work of God.

[4]*Autobiography*, pp. 325, 328-331.

Question for Thought and Prayer

If God desires to do such great things for us and for His Kingdom on earth in answer to prayer, why are my efforts and time spent on my knees so feeble?

26

PERFECTION

"The soul of a Christian, when it is burdened, must have relief. God rolls this weight upon the soul of a Christian for the purpose of bringing him nearer to himself."[1]

The *Lectures on Revivals of Religion* were preached while I was still pastor of the Presbyterian Church in Chatham Street Chapel. The two following winters, I gave lectures to Christians in the Broadway Tabernacle, which were also reported by Mr. Leavitt, and published in the *New York Evangelist*. These also have been printed in a volume in this country and in Europe.[2] Those sermons to Christians were very much the result of a searching that was going on in my own mind. I mean that the Spirit of God was showing me many things, in regard to the question of sanctification, that led me to preach these sermons to Christians.

Many Christians regarded those lectures as an exhibition of the Law rather than the Gospel. But I did not, and do not, so regard them. For me the Law and Gospel have but one rule of life, and every violation of the spirit of the

---

[1]*Principles of Prayer*, p. 36.

[2]The sermons that Finney is referring to are published in his *Lectures to Professing Christians* (London: Milner and Company, 1837). Two of these sermons with the title "Christian Perfection" on the text Matthew 5:48 have not been reprinted in any recent collection of Finney's sermons. Other sermons on sanctification can be found in his works published by Bethany House Publishers.

Law is also a violation of the spirit of the Gospel. But I have long been satisfied that the higher forms of Christian experience are attained only as a result of a terribly searching application of God's Law to the human conscience and heart. The result of my labors up to that time had shown me more clearly than I had known before, the great weakness of Christians, and that the older members of the church, as a general thing, were making very little progress in grace. I found that they would fall back from a revival state even sooner than young converts. It had been so in the revival in which I myself was converted. I now clearly that this was owing to their early teaching; that is, to the views which they had been led to entertain when they were young converts.

I was also led into a state of great dissatisfaction with my own want of stability in faith and love. To tell the truth, I must say, to the praise of God's grace, He did not suffer me to backslide, to anything like the extent to which manifestly many Christians did backslide. But I often felt myself weak in the presence of temptation, and needed frequently to hold days of fasting and prayer and to spend much time in renewing my own life in order to retain that communion with God and that hold upon the divine strength that would enable me to labor efficiently for the promotion of revivals of religion.

In looking at the state of the Christian Church, as it had been revealed to me in my revival labors, I was led earnestly to inquire whether there was not something higher and more enduring than the Christian Church was aware of; whether there were not promises and means provided in the Gospel for the establishment of Christians in altogether a higher form of Christian life. I had known somewhat of the view of sanctification entertained by our Methodist brethren. But as their idea of sanctification seemed to me to relate almost altogether to states of the sensibility (emotions), I could not receive their teaching. However, I gave myself earnestly to search the Scriptures, and to read whatever came to hand upon the subject, until my mind was satisfied that an altogether higher and more stable form of Christian life was attainable, and was the privilege of all Christians.

This led me to preach in the Broadway Tabernacle two sermons on Christian perfection.[3] Those sermons are now included in the volume of lectures preached to Christians. In those sermons I defined what Christian perfection is, and endeavored to show that it is attainable in this life, and the sense in which it is attainable. [I said these sermons were published in the *New York Evangelist*. So far as I know they did not startle the Christian Church as anything heretical, for until some time after I came to Oberlin, I never heard the question of the truth of those sermons being raised in any quarter.] But about this time, the question of Christian perfection, in the antinomian sense of the term, was heatedly discussed at New Haven, at Albany, and somewhat in New York City. I examined these views, as published in the periodical entitled *The Perfectionist*. But I could not accept them. Yet I was satisfied that the doctrine of sanctification in this life, and entire sanctification, in the sense that it was the privilege of Christians to live without known sin, was a doctrine taught in the Bible, and that abundant means were provided for the securing of that attainment.

The last winter that I spent in New York, the Lord was pleased to visit my soul with a great refreshing. After a period of great searching of heart, He brought me, as He has often done, into a new awareness of himself and gave me much of that divine sweetness in my soul, of which President Edwards speaks as attained in his own experience. That winter I had a time of thorough repentance in my own life, so much so that sometimes, for a considerable period, I

---

[3]When Finney went to Oberlin, he preached another series on perfection, and these are found in *The Promise of the Spirit*, edited by Timothy L. Smith, and published by Bethany House Publishers.

could not refrain from loud weeping in view of my own sins and of the love of God in Christ. Such seasons were frequent that winter, and resulted in the great renewal of my spiritual strength and enlargement of my views in regard to the privileges of Christians and the abundance of the grace of God.[4]

Question for Thought and Prayer

Have you ever thoroughly examined your life according to the Law of God, confessed your sins, and rejoiced that Jesus Christ has given you victory over all known sin?

---

[4]*Autobiography*, pp. 339-441.

27

TOTAL COMMITMENT

"Try the spirits by the Bible. . . . If you compare them faithfully with the Bible, you never need be led astray. You can always know whether your feelings are produced by the Spirit's influence by comparing your desires with the spirit and temper of religion as described in the Bible. . . . The Spirit of God influences the mind, . . . He enlightens the intelligence, and leads the Christian who is under His influence to be eminently reasonable and rational in all his views and movements."[1]

During the winter of 1843, the Lord gave my own soul a very thorough spiritual overhauling and a fresh baptism of His Spirit. I boarded at the Marlborough Hotel in Boston, and my study and bedroom were in one corner of the chapel building. My mind was greatly drawn out in prayer for a long time, as indeed it always has been when I have labored in Boston. I have been favored there with a great deal of the spirit of prayer. But this winter, in particular, my mind was exceedingly exercised on the question of personal holiness; in respect to the state of the church, their want of power with God; the weakness of the orthodox churches in Boston, the weakness of their faith, and their want of power in the midst of such a community. The fact that they were making little or no progress in overcoming the errors of that city greatly affected my mind.

---

[1]*Principles of Prayer*, p. 70.

I gave myself to a great deal of prayer. After my evening services, I would retire as early as I well could, but rose at four o'clock in the morning, because I could sleep no longer, and immediately went to the study and prayed. And so deeply was I exercised, and so absorbed in prayer, that I frequently continued from the time I arose at four o'clock till the gong called to breakfast at eight o'clock. My days were spent, so far as I could get time, in searching the Scriptures [for I had a great deal of company coming constantly to see me]. I read nothing else, all that winter, but my Bible; and a great deal of it seemed new to me. Again the Lord took me, as it were, from Genesis to Revelation. He led me to see the connection of things, the promises, threatenings, the prophecies and their fulfillment; and indeed, the whole Scripture seemed to me all ablaze with light, and not only light, but it seemed as if God's Word was instinct with the very life of God.

After praying in this way for weeks and months, one morning while I was engaged in prayer, the thought occurred to me, what if, after all this divine teaching, my will is not carried, and this teaching takes effect only in my sensibility? May it not be that my sensibility is affected by these revelations from the Bible and that my heart is not really subdued by them? At this point several passages of Scripture occurred to me, such as this: "Line must be upon line, line upon line, precept upon precept, precept upon precept, here a little, and there a little, that they might go and fall backward, and be snared and taken." The thought that I might be deceiving myself [by the states of my feelings], when it first occurred to me, stung me almost like an adder. It created a pain that I cannot describe. The passages of Scripture that occurred to me, in that direction, for a few moments greatly increased my distress. But directly I was enabled to fall back upon the perfect will of God. I said to the Lord that if He saw it was wise and best, and that His honor demanded that I should be left to be deluded and go down to hell, I accepted His will, and I said to Him, "Do with me as seemeth Thee good."

Just before this occurrence, I had a great struggle to consecrate myself to God in a higher sense than I had ever before seen to be my duty, or conceived as possible. I had often before laid all my family upon the altar of God, and left them to be disposed of at His discretion. But at this time that I now speak of, I had had a great struggle about giving up my wife to the will of God. She was in very feeble health, and it was very evident that she could not live long. I had never before seen so clearly what was implied in laying her, and all that I possessed, upon the altar of God. For hours I struggled upon my knees to give her up totally to the will of God. But I found myself unable to do it. I was so shocked and surprised at this that I perspired profusely with agony. I struggled and prayed until I was exhausted, and found myself entirely unable to give her altogether up to God's will in such a way as to make no objection to His disposing of her just as He pleased.

This troubled me much. I wrote to my wife, telling her what a struggle I had had and the concern that I had felt at not being willing to commit her, without reserve, to the perfect will of God. This was but a very short time before I had this temptation, as it now seems to me to have been, of which I have spoken, when those passages of Scripture came up distressingly to my mind, and when the bitterness almost of death seemed for a few moments to possess me at the thought that my faith might be of emotions only and that God's teaching might have taken effect only in my feelings. But as I said, I was enabled, after struggling for a few moments with this discouragement and bitterness, which I have since attributed to a fiery dart of Satan, to fall back in a deeper sense than I had ever done before upon the infinitely blessed and perfect will of God. I then told the Lord that I had such confidence in Him that I felt perfectly willing to give myself, my wife and my family, all to be disposed of [without any qualification] according to His own [views and will]. [That if He thought it best and wise to send me to hell, to do so, and I would consent to it. As to my wife, I felt so entirely willing to lay her body and soul upon the altar without the least misgiving in my mind in delivering her up to the perfect will of God.]

I then had a deeper view than ever before of what was implied in consecration to God. I spent a long time upon my knees in considering the matter all over, and giving up everything to the will of God: the interests of the church, the progress of Christianity, the conversion of the world, and the salvation or damnation of my own soul, as the will of God might decide. Indeed, I remember that I went so far as to say to the Lord, with all my heart, that He might do anything with me or mine to which His blessed will could consent. I had such perfect confidence in His goodness and love as to believe that He could consent to do nothing to which I could object. I felt a kind of holy boldness in telling Him to do with me just as seemed to Him good; that He could not do anything that was not perfectly wise and good; therefore, I had the best of grounds for accepting whatever He could consent to in respect to me and mine. So deep and perfect a resting in His will I had never known before.

What has appeared strange to me is this, that I could not get hold of my former hope; nor could I recollect with any freshness any of the former seasons of communion and divine assurance that I had experienced. I may say that I gave up hope and rested everything upon a new foundation. I mean, I gave up my hope from any past experience, and recollect telling the Lord that I did not know whether He intended to save me or not. Nor did I feel concerned to know. I was willing to abide the event. I said that if I found that He kept me, and worked in me by His Spirit, and was preparing me for heaven, working holiness and eternal life in my soul, I should take it for granted that He intended to save me. That if, on the other hand, I found myself empty of divine strength and light and love, I should conclude that He saw it wise and expedient to send me to hell. In either event I would accept His will. My mind settled into a perfect stillness.

This was early in the morning, and through the whole of that day I seemed to be in a state of perfect rest, body and soul. The question frequently arose in my mind during the day, "Do you still adhere to your consecration and abide in the will of God?" I said without hesitation, "Yes, I take nothing back. I have no reason for taking anything back. I went no further in oaths and promises than was reasonable. I have no reason for taking anything back. I do not want to take anything back." The thought that I might be lost did not distress me. Indeed, think as I might, during that whole day, I could not find in my mind the least fear, the least disturbing emotion. Nothing troubled me. I was neither elated nor depressed. I was neither, as I could see, joyful nor sorrowful. My confidence in God was perfect. My acceptance of His will was perfect, and my mind was as calm as heaven.

Just at evening, the question arose in my mind, "What if God should send me to hell, what then?" "Why, I would not object to it." "But can He send a person to hell," was the next inquiry, "who accepts His will in the sense in which you do?" This inquiry was no sooner raised in my mind than settled. I said, "No, it is impossible. Hell could be no hell to me if I accepted God's perfect will." This sprung a vein of joy within me that kept developing more and more, for weeks and months, and indeed I may say, for years. For years I was too full of joy to feel much exercised with anxiety on any subject. My prayer that had been so fervent, and protracted during so long a period, seemed all to run out into, "Thy will be done." It seemed as if my desires were all met. What I had been praying for, for myself, I had received in a way that I least expected. Holiness to the Lord seemed to be inscribed in all my thoughts and activities. I had such strong faith that God would accomplish all His perfect will that I could not worry about anything. The great anxieties about which my mind had been exercised during my seasons of agonizing prayer seemed to be set aside; so that for a long time, when I went to God, to commune with Him—as I did very, very frequently—I would fall on my knees and find it impossible to ask for anything, with any earnestness, except that His will might be done in earth as it is done in heaven. My prayers were swallowed up in that. I often found myself smiling, as it were, in the face of God, and saying that I did not want anything. I was very sure that He would accomplish all His wise and good pleasure, and with that my soul was entirely satisfied.

Here I lost that great struggle in which I had been engaged for so long a time, and began to preach to the congregation in accordance with this new and enlarged experience. There was a considerable number in the church, and that attended my preaching, who understood me. They saw from my preaching what had been, and what was, passing in my mind. I presume the people were more aware than I was myself of the great change in my manner of preaching. Of course, my mind was too full of the subject to preach anything except a full and present salvation in the Lord Jesus Christ.

At this time it seemed as if my soul was wedded to Christ in a sense in which I had never had any thought or conception of before. The language of the Song of Solomon was as natural to me as my breath. I thought I could understand well the state of mind he was in when he wrote that song; and concluded then, as I have thought ever since, that that song was written by him after he had been reclaimed from his great backsliding. I not only had all the freshness of my first love, but a greater appreciation of it. Indeed, the Lord lifted me so much above anything that I had experienced before, and taught me so much of the meaning of the Bible, of Christ's relations, and power, and willingness, that

I often found myself saying to Him, "I had not known or conceived that any such thing was true." I then realized what is meant by the saying that He "is able to do exceeding abundantly above all that we ask or think." He did at that time teach me infinitely above all that I had ever asked or thought. I had had no conception of the length and breadth, and height and depth, and efficiency of His grace.

It seemed then to me that the passage, "My grace is sufficient for thee," meant so much, that it was wonderful; I had never understood before. I found myself exclaiming, "Wonderful! Wonderful! Wonderful!" as these revelations were made to me. I could understand then what was meant by the prophet when he said, "His name shall be called Wonderful, Counsellor, The mighty God, The everlasting Father, The Prince of Peace." I spent nearly all the remaining part of the winter, till I was obliged to return home, in instructing the people in regard to the fullness there is in Christ. But I found that I preached over the heads of the majority of the people. They did not understand me. Thankfully, however, there was indeed a godly number that did, and they were wonderfully blessed in their souls, and made more progress in the divine life, as I have reason to believe, than in all their lives before.

As the great excitement of that season subsided and I became more calm, I saw more clearly the different steps of my Christian experience, and came to recognize the connection of things as all wrought by God from beginning to end. But since then I have never had these great struggles and long protracted seasons of agonizing prayer [before I could get hold of full rest in God] that I had often experienced. It is quite another thing to prevail with God, in my own experience, from what it was before. I can come to God with greater calmness because I come with more perfect confidence. He enables me now to rest in Him, and let everything sink into His perfect will, with much more readiness than ever before the experience of that winter.

I have felt since then a greater freedom, a buoyancy and delight in God and in His Word; a steadiness of faith, a Christian liberty and overflowing love, that I had only experienced, I may say, occasionally before. I do not mean that such experiences had been rare to me before; for they had been frequent and often repeated, but never abiding as they have been since. My bondage seemed to be, at that time, entirely broken. And since then, I have had the freedom of a child with a loving parent. It seems to me that I can find God within me in such a sense that I can rest upon Him and be quiet, lay my heart in His hand and nestle down in His perfect will and have no worry or anxiety.

I speak of these exercises as habitual since that period, but I cannot affirm that they have been altogether unbroken; for in 1860, during a period of sickness, I had a season of great depression and wonderful humiliation. But the Lord brought me out of it into an established peace and rest.[2]

Question for Thought and Prayer

Have I so committed my all to the Lord, and so consecrated myself to Him and His service, that I am willing and able to receive whatever future He intends for me from His hand?

------

[2]*Autobiography*, pp. 374-381.

28

QUENCHING THE HOLY SPIRIT

"If you have much of the Spirit of God, you must make up your mind to have much opposition, both in the church and the world. . . . Often the elders, and even the minister, will oppose you if you are filled with the Spirit of God. You must expect very frequent and agonizing conflicts with Satan. Satan has very little trouble with those Christians who are not spiritual, but lukewarm, and slothful, and worldly-minded. And such do not understand what is said about spiritual conflicts."[1]

[After spending a few weeks in Detroit in 1846, in compliance with the earnest request of the church at Pontiac, I went there for a season. At Pontiac I found a very unusual and trying state of things. The place had been settled at first by a class of infidels, who were scoffers of religion. But there were several pious women in the neighborhood; and after a great struggle, they finally prevailed to have religious meetings established, and had built a church and found a minister. There was then living in Pontiac the man who had been the pastor of the church immediately preceding the brother who was there at the time I went. The young man who was pastor when I arrived was from New England. His name I do not now recollect. With the former pastor, the church had had a great difficulty. They had become

---

[1]*Principles of Prayer*, p. 84.

very much divided in respect to him, and finally dismissed him. But the circumstances had been such as to leave a very bad state of feeling between him and the church, and also between him and another elder minister, who lived close to the village, and who had labored a good deal as a missionary in that new country in establishing churches. This former missionary had taken a very active part in the controversy between the old pastor and the church; so that between him and the old pastor there was no ministerial or even Christian sympathy. Indeed, I found the state of things about as unpromising and difficult to manage as I had ever met with anywhere. However, I began to preach, and it was soon evident that the Spirit of God was greatly searching the church. I began there, as I usually did, to have the hindrances to revival removed, mutual confession, and restitution attended to, and in short to re-convert the church and prepare the way for a general revival among the openly impenitent. The state of morals at that time in Pontiac was low.

The people were enterprising, and the place was thrifty in a business point of view; but true Christianity was at the lowest ebb. I saw that nothing effectual could be done until the old roots of bitterness were extracted, their divisions healed, and their animosities put away.

I therefore addressed my preaching to the church and to the professing Christians, and preached as boldly to them as I could. That was the home of their Lieutenant Governor Richardson. His wife was a religious woman, but had been drawn considerably into the great controversy between their old pastor and the church. After preaching for a week or two I thought the way was sufficiently prepared; and it was agreed to set apart a day for fasting, humiliation, and prayer. When the day arrived, I preached to them from this text: "Oh, the hope of Israel and the Savior thereof, why art Thou to us a stranger in the land, and as a wayfaring man that tarrieth but for a night?" I was greatly concerned with the application of this text to the present condition of that people. In the afternoon we had a general prayer meeting of the church. Soon after the meeting began, it was evident to me that the Holy Spirit was present in a powerful way. I was the guest of a Mr. Davis, who had taken a very prominent part in the controversy with their old pastor. He was a man of strong opinions, and had been most hostile in his feelings to their old pastor, placing full blame upon him. This old pastor lived a near neighbor to him. As we came home from the morning service, I saw that Mr. Davis was very deeply convicted. He said to me, "Don't you think it would be best for me to go and make confession to that minister?" "He was wrong," said he, "but I have had a very bad attitude toward him." I inquired, "Can you go and confess to him without reproaching him, leaving him to confess his own sins?" He said he could; and immediately he left the house, went over, and as I understood, made a humble confession without accusing him at all. He told him that he had entertained very unchristian feelings toward him, and asked his forgiveness.

As I said, soon after we assembled in the afternoon, it was evident that there was a spirit of great conviction on the congregation. Their old pastor was present, as I believe he was every time we had held meeting. Soon after we had assembled, I observed Mrs. Richardson rise from her seat and pass around the church to the opposite side where her old pastor sat, and openly confessed to him that she had entertained very unchristian feelings toward him. This had a remarkable effect on those present. I observed that the old pastor's face turned deadly pale. As soon as Mrs. Richardson turned away, there was quite a general movement from different parts of the house of persons going to his seat to confess to him. I saw how the work was going on, and felt confident that there would be a general humbling of those present.

From the manifest impression that it was making upon

their old pastor, I expected every moment to see him go to his knees and make confession. The pressure at this time upon the congregation was tremendous. I kept entirely still; and so also did their new pastor, the young man. But just at this moment, the old missionary, whose name I think was Ruggles, arose and objected to what was going on. He objected to it, he said, because their old pastor, calling him by name, would triumph and say that the congregation had justified him and condemned themselves. I did not believe then, nor do I now, that there was the least danger of that. I think if Father Ruggles, as they called him, had kept still, it would not have been ten minutes before the pastor would have made as full a confession as they could have desired. However, Father Ruggles was too strongly committed against the old pastor to allow anything being done that could, by any possibility, be construed into a justification of the pastor's course, and a condemnation of the course which his church had pursued toward him. The moment Father Ruggles took this position, a terrible reaction came over the meeting. All confession ceased; all tears were wiped away; and I never in any meeting in my life saw so manifest a quenching of the Holy Spirit's influence as was manifest there.

The reaction was instantaneous, terrible, and decisive. Up to that moment all their animosities were melted away, but this mistaken course of Father Ruggles brought the rising spirit of confession to a halt, totally reversed its course, and tore the old wounds open once again. After looking at the desolation for a few days, I returned to Detroit, where I was taken sick, and for a number of days confined to my bed. The season had arrived for opening our spring term at Oberlin, and as soon as I was able to travel I returned home, and as usual commenced my labors here; and we had a very interesting revival through the summer.][2]

[2]From the unpublished manuscript of the *Autobiography* between pages 385 and 386.

Question for Thought and Prayer

Through unconfessed sin and animosity, am I stifling revival in my church and hindering God from answering my prayers?

29

FINNEY'S VISION NEAR DEATH

"To be sure, God often more than answers prayer. He grants them not only what they ask, but often connects other blessings with it."[1]

[That summer (1847) I published the second volume of my *Systematic Theology*. I wrote it out and published it, and attended to my college and pastoral duties. Most of the second volume I wrote at the rate of a lecture a day, and sent it to the printers; so that I would correct the proof of one lecture, and write another and send it to the press the same day. But this, with all my pastoral duties, and my intense labors in my classes, so used up my strength, that on commencement evening I was taken with the typhus fever. For two months I was very sick, and came very, very near death. Meanwhile my precious wife was failing of tuberculosis. About the middle of December she passed away. When she died, my strength had not returned; and I stayed at home that winter, and did not perform much ministerial labor here or elsewhere. I resumed my labors as pastor and professor too soon to favor a rapid return to strength. For this reason, I remained at home through the winter of 1847-8, not feeling able to perform the labors of an evangelist abroad.]

---

[1]*Principles of Prayer*, p. 52.

NOTATIONS BY FINNEY'S WIFE DURING
HIS ILLNESS IN 1847

Wednesday, 25th August—Addressed his graduating class. Came home totally exhausted. But went out in the evening and attended a meeting of the trustees. When he came home, sat down and talked a little while with Mrs. Blake. Complained of great pain in his head and uncommon exhaustion. Rested very little during the night.

26th—Thought he would get up but found himself unable to dress, and went to bed again. Great restlessness through the day. Took nothing into his mouth, not even a drop of water.

27th—A restless night, severe pains in the head and back, and continued through the day. Said, "Oh, how sweet it would be to be undisturbed in the grave, no pain, none of this restlessness. But I can't die, I shall never die." Talked with me about the making of his will. Said that he had sometimes thought that it looked so much as though he felt the property which he held in his name was his own. But when he became sick that the law would recognize it as his. He felt that he might as well dispose of it as for the law to do it, and accordingly he got Mr. Parish of Sandusky to write it in the afternoon.

28th—Seemed more comfortable in the morning, sat up for a few moments. Still his restlessness continues. Said, "I do not want to live, I am ready to go," and with a sweet smile added, "You, my dear, will soon go too."

29th, Sabbath—His birthday. Passed a horrible night. His mind so active that he could not rest. His sleep a kind of dreamy consciousness, partly of life and partly of death. Said to the doctor, "I am a poor patient for you, for I am entirely exhausted, my strength is all gone. It seems all but impossible to get up again." Said he had thought out a great many books during the night.

30th—Evidently worse, had an awfully distressing

night, as he expressed it all night, "Sweet to be in the hands of the Lord." Said, "I don't know whether Dr. Jenning (?) is right or not; at all events, I have no confidence in any other theory. It is the best light I have." Gave directions about a great many things, what I had better do under such and such circumstances. Talked about appointing a guardian for the boys, especially little Norton. Said that every system of moral philosophy was fundamentally false.

31st—His system more quiet, slept some, P.M. When he awoke, said, "What profound rest. No words can describe the sweet peace. Thank the Lord my mind is calm, nothing is suffered to disturb its deep repose. I shall soon see William, and if we get to discussing the great subjects, we should get light fast."

With regard to a certain subject, said he had said unkind and unwise things to a few individuals. Still he looked at the facts and the developments just as he did at the time. But the Lord enabled him last winter to leave it all to the judgment and let it rest there. Said, "My dear, I have often grieved you, but I know that I have your forgiveness, and I am not troubled. Jesus saves me from all anxiety."

When I said, "Charles is no better, and Norton was most sick, and that Rebecca was unable to sit up, threatened with a fever," he said, "What a blessed thing for us all to die together. It seems to me as if I was going to die. I am making all my arrangements for those I am going to leave, though I have not thought much about the place where I am going. Still I had this morning a view of how heaven was lighted. It was imagination, I presume. But such splendid columns and palisades, their tops enveloped in such glorious light, and yet there was no sun. A little glimpse of heaven, imagination, I suppose. I don't know yet, perhaps not. Sweet Jesus, sweet Jesus, I have wanted to write more books, but how sweet this passage, 'Seal up the words of these books and write them not.' "[2]

Question for Thought and Prayer

Is my relationship with God through faith in Jesus Christ such that I could approach death, calling, "Sweet Jesus, sweet Jesus"?

---

[2]The first part of this sketch should be inserted prior to page 386 in the *Autobiography*. The account by Finney's wife appears in the back pages of one of Finney's old Pastoral Theology notebooks, believed to be of his lectures in the 1840s, catalogued 091.25, F 497 C. It is written in pencil, and is hard to read in places.

30

THE CONSEQUENCES OF APOSTASY

"If you die without the Spirit, you will fall into hell.
There can be no doubt about this. Without the Spirit you
will never be prepared for heaven."[1]

[A circumstance occurred during this revival relating to
the celebrated Theodore Parker, who held services in a
large hall in Boston, and whose views of theology and religion are so well understood that I need not enter into partic-
ulars in regard to them. During this winter, a good many
Christian people became very much exercised in their
minds about the evil influence that he was exerting in Boston, and there was much prayer offered for him. I called
twice myself to see him, hoping to have an opportunity to
converse with him; but in both instances he declined to see
me, as was declared due to the state of his health.

But the spirit of prayer for him seemed to increase, and
took on this type: that the Lord would convert him if He
wisely could; but that if He could not do this, that his evil
influence might in some way be set aside. God's people labored so much upon this point, that a number of Christian
gentlemen met by appointment in a certain place to lay this
matter before God. I state the facts as they were told me by
one of the gentlemen present. He said that after the meeting was opened, they called on one of their number to lead
in prayer; and he led out in prayer in such a remarkable

---

[1]*Principles of Prayer*, p. 91.

manner—laid the whole subject so fully before God, and in such a spirit, as to lead them all with one heart and one soul to unite in laying the whole case before God. He said the man who led in prayer seemed almost to be inspired; to say just the right things, and in the right way and spirit, in leading them in prayer.

They all felt as if their prayer would be answered; and so deep was this impression, that although they had come together for a prayer, after the first prayer was offered no one had a word to say. He said that the feeling was unanimous that they had prayed enough, that the answer to their prayer was certain, and that no more prayer was necessary; and none of them felt inclined to offer any further petition to God about it. In some way this prayer meeting came to the knowledge of Dr. Parker, and he said, and I believe wrote, some very strong things against it. However, he soon became very ill, became unable to preach, went to Europe for his health, and there died. Thus ended the evil influence of his preaching forever, except as the remembrance of it may influence future generations.][2]

Question for Thought and Prayer

When I pray, am I fully aware of the awesome power of prayer in those who are fully consecrated Christian people?

---

[2]To be inserted following page 444 in the *Autobiography*. Theodore Parker was a Unitarian preacher, born 1810—died 1860. It is of this passage in the handwritten manuscript, which was edited by Fairchild for publication, that Fairchild wrote on the manuscript, "Dear Bro. S. Read this with Bro. W. and tell me whether it should go in."

APPENDIX A

PROFESSOR WRIGHT'S OBSERVATIONS

The following observations regarding Finney's public prayer life, including some examples of his prayers, are made by G. Frederick Wright, Professor of Oberlin Theological Seminary, Oberlin, Ohio, and are taken from his biography of Finney: *Charles Grandison Finney* (Boston and New York: Houghton and Mifflin and Company, 1891), pp. 274-279. Wright's biography gives an excellent analysis of both Finney's life and theology.

Finney's prayers were always a most interesting and inspiring part of the public services at Oberlin. Apparently he prayed in public as he did in private, forgetful that any were present beside himself and his Creator. His petitions for the afflicted and needy of the parish were peculiarly touching and tender. He seemed to have every individual always before his mind. The students can never forget how, when the autumn term drew to a close, and they were about to face the trials of teaching in the winter schools throughout the region, his prayers for them would increase in fervency as he besought the Lord to keep the "dear children from misfortune and evil, and to gird them with strength for their trying work."* His petitions were entirely free from

---

*G. F. Wright's own autobiography relates very touchingly the difficulties he encountered as a winter teacher from Oberlin. These winter students had a great influence, and did spread their concern for the abolition of slavery throughout the country. See G. Frederick Wright, *Story of My Life and Work*; Oberlin: Bibliotheca Sacra Co., 1916.

formality, and were usually limited to objects of immediate interest, and only on occasions comprehended the country and the world at large. Apparently he relied much upon the direct leadings of the Holy Spirit in prayer, and this child-like spirit must be kept in mind if we would properly understand the significance of some of the immediate answers that came. Probably his aversion to uttering many of the ordinary general petitions arose from his doctrine respecting the "prayer of faith." In his lecture upon that subject he replies, in answer to the question, at what times are we to offer this prayer? "When you have evidence from promises, or prophecies, or providences, or the leading of the Spirit, that God will do the things you pray for. You have no evidence that it is God's will to convert the whole world at once."[1] Some of his remarkable prayers for rain can scarcely be accounted for except upon the explanation that he was led by the Spirit. For example:

The summer of 1853 was unusually hot and dry, so that the pastures were scorched, and there seemed likely to be a total failure of the crops. Under these circumstances, the great congregation gathered one Sabbath in the church at Oberlin as usual, when, though the sky was clear, the burden of Finney's prayer was for rain. In his prayer he deepened the cry of distress which went up from every heart by mentioning in detail the consequences of prolonged drought. It was in about these words:

"We do not presume, O Lord, to dictate to thee what is best for us; yet thou dost invite us to come to thee as children to a father and tell thee all our wants. We want rain. Our pastures are dry. The earth is gaping open for rain. The cattle are wandering about and lowing in search for water. Even the little squirrels in the woods are suffering from thirst. Unless thou givest us rain, our cattle must die, and

---

[1]*Lectures on Revivals of Religion*, p. 77.

our harvests will come to nought. O Lord, send us rain, and send it now! Although to us there is no sign of it, it is an easy thing for thee to do. Send it now, Lord, for Christ's sake! Amen."[2]

Says a correspondent,[3] in describing the remainder of the scene, "I remember, as distinctly as yesterday, the prolongation, the fervency, the urgency, the heartfelt pleadings, of those petitions. I remember that at length he closed, took his text, and preached perhaps ten or fifteen minutes, when we began to hear the patter upon the roof. I remember that he preached a few minutes longer; that the rattle and the roar increased; that suddenly he stopped and said, 'I think we had better thank God for the rain'; that when he gave out the hymn,

'When all thy mercies, O my God!
My rising soul surveys.'

that the whole congregation arose and sang it; that the rain continued, so that, when at last we were dismissed at the noon hour, multitudes stood around, and waited till the full skies could pour out their abounding floods."

At another time he prayed for rain in the following words: "O Lord, the long-looked-for clouds are at last over our heads, and we pray that they may now burst, and deluge the parched earth. Do not let them pass by and discharge their waters upon the lake, as they have done so often of late, for thou knowest, O Lord, that there is already water enough in the lake." The effect of this prayer is not related.

But occasionally his irrepressible humor came to the surface in the prayers with which he habitually closed the hour of classroom work. At one time, when for some reason the class met for a few days in his study, one or two of them yielded to the hypnotic effect of the well-cushioned seats

---

[2]Rev. Joseph Adams in *Reminiscences*, etc., pp. 55, 56.
[3]Rev. O. B. Waters.

and fell asleep. In his closing prayer, Finney did not forget these unfortunate members, but prayed that they might hereafter be kept awake. When the class came into the room the next day, they found the easy chairs replaced by hard-seated chairs from the kitchen. Finney good-humoredly remarked to them, "You see, young gentlemen, I have found a way to answer my own prayer."

At another time, when he had been dwelling at great length upon technical questions of theology, and when the danger was great of the students' getting merely the form of sound words without their power. Finney closed the hour with the prayer that the Lord would mellow their hearts, and give life and power to the truth; for, if He did not, their whole system of theology "would be so dry that it would be fit only to choke a moral agent."

On another day, when the class in theology had been quite eloquent in expressing their own views, Finney in closing prayed, "O Lord, do not let these young men think that, because they have let down a little line into the infinite sea of thy greatness, they have sounded all its depths! Save them from conceit, O Lord!"

When the National Congregational Council was organized at Oberlin, advantage was taken of its presence to dedicate the building for the theological seminary (named from the event Council Hall), though it was then but partially completed. Finney was asked to make the dedicatory prayer. Before beginning his prayer he said: "I have felt somewhat embarrassed with regard to performing this part of the service, because the house is not entirely finished. I have several times refused to take part in dedicating a house of worship that was not paid for; but this is neither finished nor paid for, and hence I have had some hesitation about offering it to God in this state. But I remember that I have often offered myself to God, and I am far from being finished yet, and why should I not offer this house just as it is? I will do so, relying upon the determination of those having it in charge to finish it as soon as possible."[4]

In general, Finney respected the rule for which he voted in the New Lebanon Convention, that it was improper to pray by name for persons in public without their permission. But I remember hearing him pray for Professor M. in a somewhat extraordinary manner, though one which unwittingly revealed his high appreciation of his associate's reputation for profundity. Finney was conducting the preliminary exercises on a Sabbath morning in which Professor M. was to preach, and he prayed that "Brother M. might be baptized with the Spirit, and might have great simplicity of speech and clearness of utterance given him, so that the great truths of the gospel should be made plain and brought within our reach, so that we should not all have to get up on tiptoe to understand what he was saying."

As a pastor, Finney attended faithfully to the spiritual functions of his office. In addition to preaching, he led the weekly prayer meeting, and held an inquiry meeting at some time during each week, and always stood ready to respond to every genuine call from those who were in spiritual trouble.

---

[4]*Oberlin News*, August 20, 1874.

APPENDIX B

A TESTIMONIAL LETTER

PRESIDENT FINNEY'S PRAYER FOR RAIN

Washington, D.C., January 1, 1912

Prof. Geo. S. Ormsby
Xenia, Ohio

My Dear Sir:

I acknowledge with pleasure your letter of 21st ultimo, in which you remind me of our meeting in this city some years since and of our conversation of Oberlin and of the "mighty man of God" who was President of the college in the long ago. You recall a poor attempt I then made to describe the man, the conditions which called for the prayer he uttered and the striking climax of the instant event, and ask that I put in writing so much of the story as may yet remain in memory.

There is no memorandum within my reach by which I can with certainty give the exact date of the occurrence; but marshalling such general facts as remain in mind, which fix the milestones in my pilgrimage of near 76 years, I conclude that it was probably when I had reached my 16th year or the summer of 1852.

From an early day in the spring time of the year the skies had withheld the rain; indeed, the curtain of the clouds was seldom drawn across the face of the sun. The

summer was passing—eyes had become wearied with looking toward the heavens for relief. The meadows gave little
hope of providing provender for the winter, the pastures
were brown and bare, the corn was cut short in its growth;
its leaves were curled and yellow as if to mock the passerby
with visions of golden ears which would never reach the
granary. The brooks had ceased to flow; their ponds had
dried up. Many wells were near exhaustion. The call on
them to share their contents with the domestic animals of
the farm had often changed "the moss-covered bucket" into
a dried out and leaking receptacle, which if sent down too
often found no answer to its quest. If one ventured into the
pasture-field, the grazing beasts ceased their search for food
and followed one about as if asking pity and relief. In those
days the farms had been but partially cleared of the giant
trees which covered the earth's floor in all that region when
pioneers of Oberlin College threaded their way to the spot
where is now the college campus, the stately buildings and
the dear old church where President Finney so long
preached and prayed.

At the time of which I write, the wild things of the woods
still found ample food and shelter on the borders of the
cleared fields. The woods were alive with squirrels. The rac-
coon and the opossum still sheltered there. In this day of
distress they forgot their fear of man and following the
fences were found about the houses and out-buildings, and
so heedless of the man and his dog that many of the squirrel
kind were killed with sticks and stones in the hands of passing boys. The grasshopper adding its burden as of old was
there in unwonted numbers, and the creeping things,
"whose day is the nighttime," came out with the sun to be
trodden under foot of man. The face of the earth was
seamed with cracks; its mouths were open for refreshing. I
have given you this partial recital of conditions that you
may better understand allusions in the prayer, some of
which I recall, and will set down.

At the time I am writing of, I was a boy farmhand, living and laboring a little less than two miles from the Old Church at Oberlin. The Sunday school assembled within its walls at 9 o'clock a.m. I was a regular attendant. As I wended my dusty way thitherward that Lord's Day morning, there was no sign of relenting in the skies. "The heavens were as brass." The school dismissed, the congregation began to gather for the morning service. The organ welcomed them. There was a great choir gathered about it. The seats were well filled. There were hundreds of serious people facing the pulpit, when Professor Morgan—dear Old John Morgan—whose ever-present smile was a benediction, mounted its steps. Then followed President Finney, a man of noble mold in both face and figure. He was in the fullness of his powers, and was, as many then thought and I still think, the greatest preacher of his day. The sun was shining. His house was but a short distance away, but he carried an umbrella to his seat. There were smiles, I am sure, at this. I know of one who smiled at the seeming unequal challenge of the Providence which ruled the hour. The service proceeded in order. The opening prayer was uttered by Professor Morgan, then came the voice of song; and when it died away, the President took his place to confess the sins of the people, to voice their distress, and to plead for mercy. There was great charm in this man. Nature set before her most skillful artificers the task of molding his form: His voice had the heart-melody of a mother when calling an erring child to a better way. His vision sometimes seemed to catch the dawning of "the day of days"; the oncoming to the judgment of all whose feet had ever trod the earth. In such moments standing in the midst of the platform pulpit, his foot advanced, his head thrown back, he looked in attitude and demeanor a Jupiter not dispensing the rains nor guiding the thunderbolts, but heaven's chief herald ordering the trumpet blast that should rend the hiding places of all the living and of all the dead, one could fancy he heard an echo of the voice of the prophet of Galilee saying "Our Father"—and so that day he spoke with the Father. And first, as always, remembering the great body of students sitting before him, he commended them to heaven's care, and especially that their feet might never stray from the straight and narrow path. Then giving liberty of speech to the chief burden of the hour, he spoke of the cloudless sun, of inanimate nature, instead of her summer garb of glory, wearing the habiliments of woe; of leaves shriveled and falling; that no flower reflected the smile of the Eternal to give his children joy, that the night was a glad shelter from a sun whose rising gave no promise of good but whose darkening shadows gave merciful relief to eyes weary of looking on "the abomination of desolation." Then he spoke with the Father of living things, the work of his own hands. How the wild things of the woods, forgetting their fear of man, sought His habitation; that the creeping things whose day is night wandered abroad in the morning to be trodden under foot of man and beast. He told the *All Merciful* of the cattle wandering over fields "which yielded no meat," looking reproachfully into men's faces as if to inquire for what sin of theirs they were so sorely afflicted, and voicing the universal cry of things animate and inanimate, his cheeks moistened with tears, he exclaimed, "Even the thirsty earth opens its mouth wide and cries to God for water!" He told of the prophet's joy, when the cloud no greater than a man's hand challenged the sun, and with filial confidence bespoke the coming blessing.

The Amen had not ceased its echo, the suppliant still stood at the desk, when with a crash and a roar resounding from the roof of the great church, a flood of rain descended. In broken accents he said, "The Lord heard whilst we were yet speaking." And the choir, with every voice in the congregation attuned to song, burst forth with Luther's glad anthem "Praise God from whom all blessings flow."

In later years I have now and then related this incident

of the long ago to ears, some in a receptive and some in a critical mood. The younger auditors no doubt wondered how so much of the memory could remain after the lapse of many years, and some inclined to raise a *quaere* about miracle and special providence.

Perhaps in those days the Christian peoples dwelt too much on a "wrestling Jacob." Perchance in these later years our vision is so occupied with the "Eternal plan" that we lose touch with the *Father's hand*. However this may be, you and I, who are upon the borderline, know how vividly old-time memories come to those who sit in the lengthening shadows of the present, and how pleasant to us are all the gleams of the past which speak of God's goodness, though dispensed with a chastening hand.

Wishing you all happiness in this New Year.

Faithfully yours,
S. S. Burdett

APPENDIX C

CHARLES GRANDISON FINNEY

A BIOGRAPHICAL SKETCH

The son of a Revolutionary War veteran, Charles G. Finney was born on August 29, 1792, in Warren, Connecticut. His lack of religious education and upbringing resulted from the general decline of Christian and biblical teaching in America following the war. True, there were times of revival in the early 1800's, but Finney was not raised in a Christian home, and he never heard a prayer in his father's house. His father did become a Christian after Finney, as an adult, presented the gospel to him.

Finney was highly gifted, intellectually, culturally and physically. Mostly self-educated, he became a school teacher, then, when twenty-six years old, he became an apprentice in the law office of Benjamin Wright in Adams, New York. He had been told that he could study law independently and pass the bar exam in two years, half the time that it would take to attend Yale.

While studying for his bar exam, and during his preparation for court cases, Finney discovered that the foundation for American law was the Bible, that American law appealed to the Bible as its absolute standard for law. So, he bought his first Bible to help him study law. He meticulously looked up each biblical reference in his law books to study it in its proper biblical context. This study of the law on the one hand and of the Bible on the other convinced him the Bible was indeed God's Word. He was weighed in the balance, and knew that he needed to attend to the state of his soul, to either go to Christ for salvation or continue living a worldly and selfish life deserving of God's judgment.

Finney was known in Adams as a despiser of religion, even though he used his considerable musical talent to direct the young people's choir at church. He sometimes attended prayer meeting, but his pastor told the church he despaired of Finney's conversion. Nevertheless, the Word and the Spirit of God were doing their work, and on October 10, 1821, Finney gave his life willingly and completely to Jesus Christ, taking Him as Lord and Savior, resolving to leave the practice of law to plead Christ's cause.

Finney's theological understanding grew rapidly through his reading of the Bible, much prayer, and heated discussions with his hyper-Calvinist pastor, George Gale, a Princeton graduate. Gale and Finney engaged in heavy theological debates, and Gale finally adopted Finney's views, though some years later.

Charles Finney was licensed to preach on December 30, 1823, at the age of 31, and became a Presbyterian missionary, traveling throughout the Western District of New York. Revivals immediately accompanied his preaching. Having been trained for the bar, he preached for a verdict as he took God's side against the sinner, expecting people to repent of their sins and come out on the Lord's side *immediately*. He preached the justice of God in love, explained the purpose of the atonement, and many from all classes of society became Christians.

In 1824 he married Lydia Andrews, but shortly after their marriage revival broke out as a result of his preaching and they had to be separated for six months. Lydia died in 1847. He then married a widow, Elizabeth F. Atkinson, a woman who provided much help in his revivals, but she died in 1863. His third wife, Rebecca Rayl, survived him, living to 1907.

Finney's success in promoting revivals prompted him to give a series of lectures that later became the famous book, *Lectures on Revivals of Religion*. This book has sold in the millions; remaining in print for almost 150 years, and having been translated into other languages. These lectures and his

Autobiography have inspired revivals around the world. When his *Lectures on Revivals of Religion* were published in England, revivals broke out almost immediately at the application of his principles. English churchmen convinced him to make two revival tours of the United Kingdom, and here he saw the same success he had seen in America. It is reported that in 1905–1906, a book detailing his revivals and revival methods inspired a great revival in China.

Finney's principles can have the same result today when, in obedience to the Holy Spirit, people read and apply the biblical truths Finney discovered and revealed in a new, challenging way. As one old Norwegian evangelist always advised: "To keep the revival fires burning in your heart, read from the Book of Acts and from Charles Finney everyday."

One of Finney's most famous revivals was in Rochester, New York, in 1830. Of that revival, the great preacher Lyman Beecher said, "That was the greatest work of God, and the greatest revival of religion, that the world has ever seen, in so short a time. One hundred thousand were reported as having connected themselves with churches as the result of that great revival. This is unparalleled in the history of the church, and of the progress of religion." Beecher had at one time opposed Finney's work, saying, "You mean to come into Connecticut, and carry a streak of fire to Boston. But if you attempt it, as the Lord liveth, I'll meet you at the state line, and call out the artillerymen, and fight every inch of the way to Boston, and I'll fight you there." Later, Finney and Beecher worked closely together for a revival in Boston, and he was to compare Finney favorably with one of their contemporaries, Asahel Nettleton, saying, "Nettleton 'sets snares' for sinners, but Finney rode them down with a cavalry charge."

In addition to his revival labors, Finney held three pastorates. In 1833, he pastored the Chatham Street Chapel in New York City. In 1835, he divided his time between teaching at Oberlin College, Oberlin, Ohio (a school he helped to found), and serving as pastor of the Broadway Tabernacle in New York City (a building he helped design). He became pastor of the Oberlin Congregational Church in 1837, a position he held for the next 35 years.

Finney became famous for his revivals while still a young man, and later he became a noted systematic theologian. Results of his preaching prove his theology worked. People became Christians when they heard him preach, and records indicate 85% of his converts remained true to their profession of faith. Likewise, thousands have since studied and applied his theology in their own ministry with similar results, whether they were evangelists, preachers, pastors, or lay people seeking to obey God's call to evangelize the world.

His lectures on theology are still available in his two books, *The Heart of Truth* and *Finney's Systematic Theology*, both published by Bethany House. *The Heart of Truth* should be read first.

Reading the collections of Finney's sermons in *Principles of Victory, Principles of Liberty*, and *Principles of Holiness* is the best introduction to his thought on both biblical and theological subjects. Most of Finney's early followers learned of him first through his sermons, and then were mentally and spiritually prepared to grapple with his systematic theology. This can be our approach today.

My theological education had so educated me away from common sense that I could not understand his *Systematic Theology* when I first began to read it. It was not until I had read many of his sermons and had the help of the Holy Spirit in prayer that the light shined. And the labor of studying Finney's theology was well worth the cost. The editor of one English edition of Finney's *Lectures on Systematic Theology* wrote: "The Editor frankly confesses, that when a student he would gladly have bartered half the books in his library to have gained a single perusal of these Lectures; and he cannot refrain from expressing the belief, that no young student of theology will ever regret the purchase or perusal of Mr. Finney's Lectures."

Prayer was one of the most important reasons for Finney's success. He did everything in a spirit of prayer. He prayed for divine guidance in reading the Scriptures, preaching, teaching, writing, his work as an evangelist, and even his praying. While Finney was lecturing to students at Oberlin College, a student once asked him a question about a passage in the Bible. Finney confessed he did not know the answer, immediately knelt down in prayer before the class, and soon rose with a glowing face to give the answer the Lord had shown him. Some classes became actual prayer meetings, when the class subject was sometimes set aside to attend to the spiritual state of the students. At other times he would go to a student's room for a time of private prayer with the student.

Finney served as President of Oberlin College from 1851–1866. His presence at the college from its beginning insured its success, as students wanted to come and learn how to do the work of an evangelist from Mr. Finney. He had insisted that blacks and women be admitted to the college on an equal basis when it was founded, and Oberlin became the first co-educational college in America. His popularity was still strong in 1851, for in his first year as President enrollment sky-rocketed from 571 to 1,070 students.

Finney was strong and vigorous to the end of his life. He resigned his pastorate shortly before his death, but continued to preach and teach on occasion until he died from a heart attack on August 16, 1875.

I became a Bible-believing Christian after I read some of Charles G. Finney's books, and found in them the answers to certain theological questions that had plagued me. At this same time I had been studying the works of Francis A. Schaeffer, whose writings answered certain crucial philosophical questions. I owe my salvation to a loving God, Who sent His Son to save me from sin, and Who sent His Holy Spirit to guide me into the truth of His Word. And I thank God for the writings of Charles Finney and Francis Schaeffer. I believe both men were called by God to be men of their time, that each man became the greatest proponent of evangelical Christianity in his own century, and that the works of both will have lasting significance, saving many lives.

People such as Gordon Olson have spent a lifetime researching Finney's ideas and making these available to others in a significant and contemporary way. Organizations such as Bethany Fellowship (with its missionary school and Bethany House Publishers), Bible Research Fellowship, and the Omaha Bible School have remained strong as they have adhered to the biblical and theological principles of Charles Finney, and as they have applied them in practical ways. L'Abri Fellowship remains a lasting memorial to Francis Schaeffer, and his work also will be continued.

If we will take the time *to study* both of these great Christian thinkers, *and apply* what we learn from them (as they each correct the other in our thinking), then we will develop our understanding of the Christian gospel in such fullness that the Holy Spirit will bless our endeavors for the kingdom of God and for the salvation of souls.

As we study the Bible and theology in preparation for our ministry, whether we are clergy or lay people, let us not push aside the centrality of prayer in maintaining our relationship with God. Finney warns all of us:

"I am convinced that nothing in the whole Christian religion is so difficult, and so rarely attained, as a praying heart. Without this you are as weak as weakness itself. If you lose your spirit of prayer, you will do nothing, or next to nothing, though you had the intellectual endowment of an angel. If you lose your spirituality, you had better stop and break off in the midst of your preparations, and repent and turn to God, or go about some other employment, for I cannot contemplate a more loathsome and abominable object than an earthly-minded minister. The blessed Lord deliver and preserve His dear church from the guidance and influence of men who know not what it is to pray."

For the sake of His kingdom,

L. G. Parkhurst